The Letter of Love

A Guide to Unconditional Love
the Soul's Purpose &
Human Energy Connection

Linda Hargesheimer

12\11

To My Husband,

who has given me the gift

of space, so I could

grow spiritually

Table of Contents

Cover Symbolism

The shining light from above, which encircles the heart,
symbolizes the Higher Power and soul as one.

The heart is faceted with the colors of the chakras,
the body's energy centers.

The inner heart is filled with the soul's transformation
to total, unconditional love.

The shadow portrays the individual's soul
as it reflects to the world.

Acknowledgments

My journey to this point has evolved with the help of so many people. Strangely enough, I will begin by thanking those who politically undermined my job. Without this turn of events in my life, I would have never come to this spiritual center or received *The Letter of Love*.

Thank you to the many teachers along the way who moved me farther along my path. They are Sylvia Plourde, Harriet Gurney, Louise Hay, Patricia Crane, and Lea Brit.

My deepest appreciation to Kathy Luke for providing me a safe space where I could open to The Group.

Thank you to Fran Lenzo, a special gift in my life, who generously shared her mountain of knowledge on printing and publishing. Peter Mars, Marsha Kramer, and Reverend Heidi Chamberlain gave me the encouragement and insight I needed at the correct time. Reverend V. P. Matthews, thank you for being a special resource.

Also thanks to all my readers who gave me insights as to where I needed to ask The Group for more clarification. Your comments were most appreciated. They included Bonnie Scarpelli, Linda Lucas, Irene Bellfy, Phillipa Morrison, Jill Batura, Kent Hargesheimer, Jennifer Whitney, and Anita LaChappelle.

Extra thanks go to my editor, Maggie Warren. Also thank you to Wade Moody, Dallas Van Koll, Jan Kolenda, Linda Johnston, and Judi Jones whose technical expertise translated my illustrations, cover idea, and text into reality.

To my husband, Philip, I give a special thanks for living through my evolution and the creation of *The Letter of Love* from meditation to publication.

To my soul that chose this life's challenges and path, so I could assist others in their soul growth, thank you. You've given me a goal larger than what I could have dreamt.

Foreword

The Letter of Love is a book for the discerning reader, one whose mind is open to exploration and is not trapped by the confines of strict religious dogma. This book was written to augment one's belief system, for it reveals the benefits of meditation when applied to a foundation based upon one's faith. The author, Linda Hargesheimer, takes the reader into the metaphysical arena to expand one's comprehension of the spiritual world. She shares an insight that reflects the similarities of ideas discovered by many people who have realized that there is more to humankind than is readily seen. For this, there is credible proof. Sociologists, psychologists and neurologists all agree that human beings use less than 3 percent of the brain's potential, and that its capability is phenomenal. It is toward this expansion of mind that *The Letter of Love* lends itself.

The Letter of Love blends the accepted with the mysterious, all in a positive way, which creates for the reader a feeling of comfort and understanding in a world filled with distress and challenge.

— Peter Mars, minister and author of *The Chaplain*

List of Illustrations

For the sake of clarity, most illustrations are shown with only one chakra connection.

Introduction

There are three kinds of people in this world: those who say, "I don't have a problem"; those who say, "I have a problem, but I don't want to deal with it"; and those who say, "I have a problem; I am going to find a way to fix it." I am the third kind.

Until 1980, I felt that I had been on a typical life journey of exploration and growth. That year, my job as the public relations director of a holding company was politically undermined by five of seven vice presidents out to eliminate the person who hired me, the president of the company. After I quit, I began a process of healing my self-esteem, learning assertiveness with authority figures, and trying to answer the question, "Why are we alive?" Since that time, answering this question has been a lifelong quest.

I began my search with an article in the Sunday magazine section of a New England newspaper about a simple American woman, Virginia Tighe, alias Ruth Simmons. During a 1950's therapy session, she was hypnotized and taken back or regressed to her childhood. While she was in a regressed state, she called herself Bridie Murphy and began talking in an Irish brogue about her life in Ireland during the 1790s. In 1956, her story brought the concept of reincarnation to the American public for the first time.

The Letter of Love

Although I had read this story before, this time the article spurred me to explore more. It led me to books on regression, reincarnation, past lives, karma, meditation, near-death experiences, color, crystals, various religions, and more. This personal investigation inspired an insatiable quest for knowledge.

Over the years, I have read many spiritual concepts that I could not accept into my belief system. As I expanded my knowledge, I have come to accept more. However, I always evaluated a concept in relation to my judgment. To date, I do not wholeheartedly accept all spiritual concepts I encounter.

In the meantime, in an effort to continually heal myself, I went to a traditional therapist, took self-esteem seminars, read self-help books, took an assertiveness class, and went on trips to the Yucatan, Egypt, Peru, and Brazil to expand my spiritual knowledge.

For a few months, I went to a spiritual therapist whose eventual purpose was to connect me to these energies. She used meditation, dream work, and drumming as primary sources of gathering information and energy release.

After I grounded myself (the act of visually attaching to the Earth and protecting myself during a meditative session), instead of working on the area of healing the therapist and I first discussed, I began a meditation similar to a vision quest, a personal interaction between a person and spirit.

Introduction

My vision included sitting on top of a pinnacle in an American desert and being visited by various animals — an eagle, a snake, and an owl. The eagle tore out the fear from my chest; the snake opened my chakra energy centers; the owl replaced my eyes with love and spiritual understanding. I was told that my mission was to teach love by speaking, writing books, and teaching classes.

The next meditation opened the chakras with a series of movements. My therapist said it looked like a Buddhist religious ritual. In the following session's meditation, I saw a large energy, outlined like a person emerging from the distance. It joined a group waiting for it. They were gathered together and looked like a group of people seen from a high ladder. None of them looked like people, with faces and clothing. Rather, each one looked like a rounded outline of a body, like the drawings you will find later in **The Letter of Love**. *As the larger energy came forward and sat, the group surrounded it. This central energy became their speaker. I was not given a name.*

At first, the words that came simultaneously to my mind and out of my mouth seemed to be Asian in origin. I didn't know what they meant. Then my therapist requested the energy to speak in our English language. It took a bit of an adjustment, but I clearly commenced to receive information. I began writing and then audio recording what I was receiving.

The Letter of Love

The information that I received deals with our soul growth from this Earth experience and our quest to release our issues, so we may become unconditionally loving. Once our full potential is achieved, we no longer have to reincarnate as humans.

The Letter of Love is the information I received. Wherever I have a personal question, or have been asked by the energy to give examples, that portion of the text will be in italics. The plain text is the received information. Often, they know what I am thinking and will answer my questions before I even verbalize them.

I have been asked by people who I think this group is. Various psychics have told me I would work with another to write a book. At the time, I never knew what kind of book. Finally, one of them told me I would be working with The Great White Brotherhood, a group of saints, sages, and ascended masters of all ages from every nation, race and religion who have united with God and comprise the heavenly host.

When I meditate, I sit in a comfortable chair with a candle lit. After praying, grounding, and protecting myself visually, I begin to breathe deeply and relax. I feel my energy slow down and expand; my whole body feels lighter and I receive the vision I described previously. I am conscious of what is going on around me and am able to start my tape recorder at the appropriate time. Sometimes the energies begin with a greeting or a discussion of some of the issues in my life. Most often they plunge right into the messages they wish to convey.

Introduction

The Letter of Love is for all people, but the energies I contact use examples from my life to illustrate points. They also use my questions as a format to express information.

The following is an example of how they speak.

In part, you are worried that what we are saying is much of what you currently believe. You believe information only after it has been worked out in your brain.

Remember when you learned to sail, you understood the concept, because sailing made sense in your brain. You take in information, but you do not automatically believe it. You absorb information slowly, until you decide whether you can believe it or not. Then you say, "Yes, this is possible. Yes, I understand it. It makes sense; I accept this into my belief system." Or you say, "This is very unusual, but I will deal with this at a future time, maybe better than I am dealing with it now."

There are many aspects of spirituality you believe now that you had no idea you would have believed years and years ago. You are open to evaluating concepts, but not "running to accept everything."

You are the same way with people. You look at them and evaluate, then you ask, "Can I get along with them?

Can I work with them? Am I comfortable around them? Can they be friends?" If so, they become close friends.

What we tell you is true. Some of this has been said for generations. This is not necessarily new information. This is information that is being progressed along many lines and through various forms, because many need to hear.

When you do the meditation before our sessions, you see many energies, not just one. We are all here to give you information. We are but a few that are available to you as you progress and distribute the information.

You wonder if there is anything else to say. There is much more to say. You must realize that this information is minimal compared to what is coming in the future.

You worry about things in your life right now, which is causing you additional stress. Things are going along fine. You need to understand that everything will be all right.

The messages I receive are direct, simple, and honest. Yes, some of this information is what I believe, but some was a total surprise. **The Letter of Love** *is about the soul and how our energetic connections can bring us closer or lead us farther away from the goal of unconditionally loving others and ourselves.*

The Letter of Love *is arranged according to the chakra colors. The energies assume that you already know the chakras, spiritual energy centers of the body, and their meaning.* **Figure 1**

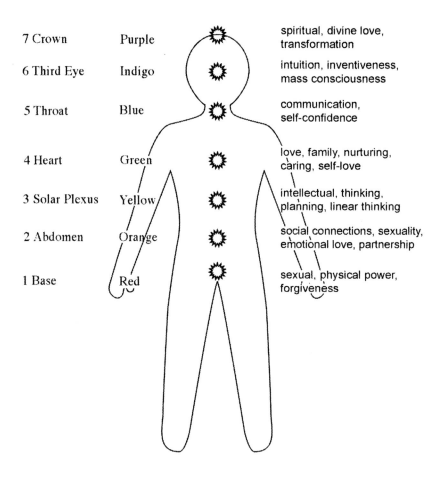

7 Crown	Purple	spiritual, divine love, transformation
6 Third Eye	Indigo	intuition, inventiveness, mass consciousness
5 Throat	Blue	communication, self-confidence
4 Heart	Green	love, family, nurturing, caring, self-love
3 Solar Plexus	Yellow	intellectual, thinking, planning, linear thinking
2 Abdomen	Orange	social connections, sexuality, emotional love, partnership
1 Base	Red	sexual, physical power, forgiveness

Figure 1 – Major Chakras

is available for clarification and referral. Most of the time, chakras are defined by colors, crystals, or areas in need of healing. Rarely are they described in relation to real-life usage, as in **The Letter of Love.**

The Letter of Love

Generally, one chakra area predominately influences your viewpoint of life. Sometimes events in your life move you among your chakras. For example, if you lose your job and live mainly in your red chakra, you ask, "How am I going to survive?" If you come from your orange chakra, you question, "How will my spouse react?" If you abide in your yellow chakra, you analyze, "What were the signs this was coming?" If you exist in the green chakra, you figure out, "How can I make this easier for my family?" If you dwell in your blue chakra, you wonder, "How do I rebuild my self-confidence?" If you inhabit your indigo chakra, you examine, "How have others survived job loss?" Finally, if you occupy your purple chakra, you surmise, "There must be something else for me to do somewhere."

Also, there will be times when I use the word, "person," and follow it with either he or she. The pronouns are interchangeable. The names of the people mentioned have been changed, but the incidents are factual. I have defined many spiritual words in the text and in a glossary in the back of the book for your convenience. If you would prefer to use the book as a tool of self-exploration, study questions are found in the back of the book.

Although I define my Higher Power as God, you should feel free to substitute Jehovah, Higher Power, Allah, The Oneness, or any other deity you would rather use in place of God. When I use a reference to God, it is followed by He. Formerly, I believed God was neither male nor female, but androgynous. Currently, I am of the opinion that God is an energy. Although writers, including myself, describe God as having human emotions, I do not believe God has human traits. God, to me, is beyond our description. Also, for the sake of clarity, most illustrations are shown with only one chakra connection. Sentences throughout the text are bolded for emphasis.

*I am not asking you to accept everything in **The Letter of Love.** Instead, please look at it, evaluate it, and decide for yourself whether it rings true to you.*

*I hope you enjoy **The Letter of Love.***

Chapter One

The Chakras and Relationships

Dear Ones—

There are many kinds of love—the love between a man and wife, the love between friends, the love between parents and children, and the love of mankind. Each is very similar and yet very different.

Love between a man and a woman is romantic, sexual, and platonic. This is most wondrous, because each level can be felt differently and simultaneously. When your emotions are in an elevated romantic state, love feels wonderful. Romantic love is wondrous for people. Everyone wants love and expects to love. A mood or setting can enhance feelings, but a genuine romantic relationship requires feeling, touching, and emotional bonding to exist.

A love connection integrates the auric energy field surrounding the human body, the chemicals of love emitted, the chakra connections, and the emotional bonds. Therefore, romantic love is the joining of two energy systems. Positive people extend their loving chakras equally toward other people **Figure 2**. They join in the heart and the spiritual energy centers, also known as

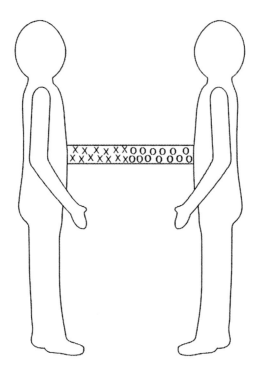

Figure 2 – Equal Energy between People

chakras. **People involved in romantic love see each other for what they are not, as well as for what they are.** The truth of who they are is not often seen in romantic love. The romantic type of love is very important for people to experience. When they do, they can then more fully understand other aspects of love.

Not all romantic love includes chemistry, which is an energy exchange between two souls who were joined in a previous past life, a time a soul lived during other incarnations on Earth. Chemistry is experienced when these same two souls meet again in this lifetime. When they are together, they feel a magnetic draw from past lifetimes. Chemistry is very, very powerful.

Chemistry includes a physical and chemical reaction. The physical comes from the magnetic energy within and around the body. It is an attraction of the chakras and the aura, the energy field surrounding the human body. The initial connection, whether positive or negative, comes from a past life. If the relationship was a positive one in a previous life, it will continue to be positive during this life.

Even though a strong attraction is felt in this lifetime, if the previous lifetime's experience was a negative relationship, the current relationship will evolve negatively. This type of chemistry is difficult to overcome, as it was for your friend, Deidra. When she was a teen, she had a romantic, chemistry attraction to her boyfriend. Since he was a negative person, their relationship turned negative.

Negative chemistry experienced again in this lifetime can motivate the person to leave the relationship. The separation must be strong and final. It is very important that the person remove herself from the relationship, so her soul can grow. Doing so means the person and her soul have progressed.

Relationships

In a relationship of only sex, just the two lower chakra energy centers connect, which is a physical attraction of the first and the second chakras. It is extremely important to understand that this is merely on the physical level and has nothing to do with the other chakras. If the upper chakra levels are involved, the relationship would continue in a loving way.

It is true that men are more attracted to physical appearance than women. Women's heart chakras and head chakras are much closer to their sexual chakras. Men's sexual chakras are more independent. When men and women join, women need their chakras to blend with compatible wavelength, auric energy.

When two people come together, they combine their energy centers. The self-confidence level is a major connection between people in either a romantic or platonic relationship. Mutual self-confidence encourages growth for the other person. When self-confidence is lacking in one partner, the other can easily discourage his partner's pursuit of goals.

The platonic bonding of a man and a woman, one in which it is assumed there is no sexual desire, is a blending of the upper chakras, not just the heart chakra. The heart chakra plays a very minor role in a platonic relationship. There is a blending of the heart, throat, and intuition chakras between friends.

A platonic partnership is wonderful because it is more equal than a romantic relationship. It is more balanced in understanding and growth. In the platonic relationship, the heart creates a bond, but it is not an emotional one. The second chakra connects more as a partnership bond. It bonds solidly in a friendship relationship, even those of men to women.

Often, the platonic relationship changes because one person or the other extends her caring or heart chakra in a major way, so feelings grow. As those feelings become more sexual, they may turn romantic. They evolve, one into the other, and they are interchangeable from one minute to the next. This is why the relationship between a man and a woman is highly challenging. Sometimes it is on a romantic feeling level, sometimes it is on a sexual, physical level, and sometimes it is on a platonic level. This does not mean one is better than another; this is just how relationships work.

Chapter Two

Red Level Energy

Physical sex, release, forgiveness, power, physical astuteness, action

Chakras and Physical Activities

When you are expressing and extending yourself physically, such as in running a demanding marathon, your base chakra extends far out to assist you. As you become exhausted from running, your base chakra begins to recede. This is when the connection between the spiritual and base chakras becomes important. If your desire to complete the marathon remains, the spiritual chakra extends itself even farther and pulls out the base chakra again. The spiritual, intuitive, and emotional chakras work together to assist the base chakra in completing the marathon.

If you are working and extending yourself in the area of art, you are using your intuitive and spiritual chakras in conjunction with your emotional chakra energy. All extend into the picture as the artist works. **Art is the expression of the artist's emotions.** Great artists extend their chakra energies magnificently into their paintings.

Master artists connect wonderfully, not only with the emotional chakra but also with spiritual, intuitive, and fine dexterity chakras. The fine dexterity of the hand comes from the lowest chakra. All of these chakras were directly connected in the great masters.

Abstract artists connect more emotionally with their work. The intuitive chakra is used for the overall design; the emotional chakra is shown by movement of line. The use of color comes from the intuitive and emotional centers.

Love of Objects

Your family influences some of your preferences for objects. Primarily, the love of objects activates your first chakra, the sexual center, to create physical excitement. This attraction also energizes a small amount of your heart center and your spiritual center, which brings a strong attraction from present or past life connections.

When people are enamored with objects, their sexual center easily becomes involved. Their energy connects from the sexual center to the crown chakra, like a bowstring. Even though we may not recognize love of objects as a sexual attraction, we become sexually stimulated by them. *For example, let's say you collect antique blue dishes. In a store, you find one and become excited. Your sexual, heart, and crown chakras are stimulated. Finding a blue dish for a person who doesn't collect them and is just looking for a blue dish would be less emotional, sexual, and past life connected.*

Everything has energy, even inanimate objects. But love is only returned from humans, not from objects. **Becoming too enamored with objects is not positive for your soul's growth. It inhibits you from your real work — connecting unconditionally to people.**

Love of Job

When you love your job, it fulfills you in many ways. Even when you do not make a lot of money, if you love your job, working is good for you. If people worked at jobs that they loved, it would be best. People would be healthier and happier.

Often, people work for many hours at jobs they dislike. Since so much of their life revolves around their jobs, their lives become more difficult and tainted by unhappiness. Sadly, over time, this unhappiness affects their physical well-being and family relationships.

Sometimes people have jobs they loved in the past but now are "burned out." For them, it is important to recognize their feelings and leave. If they stay, their bodies will create physical issues, ranging from depression to major illness.

It is important to recognize whether you are happy or unhappy with your job. Even if leaving is scary, an unhappy person needs to find another position for her own well-being and her soul's growth.

Sex and the Body

Sex is a form of love of the body. When sex is shared, it is very special. Amenable feelings are required for a positive sexual experience.

Even though a person is not in a committed sexual relationship, God does not judge a person negatively. Loose sex does not defile you. God loves everyone.

Sometimes there is an unwise and loose sharing of bodies for sex. If the partners are not lovingly compatible, sex disrupts their energies. **Sexual energy leaves the body at a rate based on the intensity of the sexual experience.** Generally, sex will not destroy the body energies, but it may not be compatible with the body. If the sexual act was intense, the energy will often take two or three days to leave the body. If the sex was just a coupling, the energy will leave within 24 hours. A positive sexual feeling, however, stays longer with a person.

The emotional intent of a person also affects the actual physical coupling. Married or committed coupling is intense because the energy is initially strong. The energy continues to vibrate in the body much longer, because of the personal commitment.

When a person is in a committed relationship, over time, the initial heightened sexual feeling diminishes. It becomes comfortable. This does not mean the couple is not in love; it means the love has moved to a different level. This is an important progression of love for the body. Remaining in a state of intense sexual attraction 24 hours a day would rapidly exhaust the body's energy.

If a couple falls out of love, the sexual coupling is not intense. It becomes just an act.

Chakras and People Who Do Not Love

Currently, there are a number of children being born who cannot love. Their energy has been affected by drugs, alcohol, etc., taken by their parents prior to copulation. The emotional energies of both parents combine to form the child's emotional makeup. Later the soul, that has chosen to overcome this challenge, joins the merged energy. These children are not here to love. Since they do not know how to love, they are selfish.

Children born without a conscience are here to teach their parents and society a lesson. If you traced the parents' emotions at conception, you would find rage. This is unfortunate.

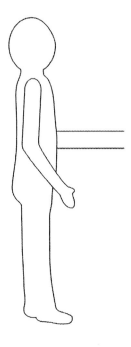

Figure 3 – Positive Person's Chakra

People's positive chakra areas extend from the body like a thick trunk **Figure 3**. The chakras of children who cannot love do not extend typically; instead they project like a thin branch out and then return to the body **Figure 4**. Their previous lifetime issues were so traumatic that they have come to learn love and joy so that they can heal.

Figure 4 – Children Who Cannot Love

It is a huge challenge for these children. Sometimes they will go two or three lifetimes before they will totally release and learn to love.

Why are children born who can't control their angry behavior?

Copulation again. During copulation rage was felt. If both parents felt it, the child will be totally out of control. If it were just the father or just the mother, anger will be an

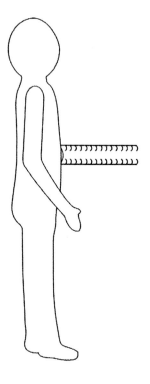

Figure 5 – Children Who Do Not Feel

issue, but not totally out of control. For children who do not feel, the edges of the chakras peel inward to destroy its root **Figure 5**.

These are people who formerly had chakra connections, but because of lack of self-love or a variety of life events, they feel negative or do not have connective feelings. Generally their chakra energy centers peel outward from the root, leaving a narrower connection.

A life changing or awakening experience may resolidify those chakras. The change may also be triggered by a shock or from being lonely. Some people even separate themselves from others.

Everybody needs friendship or other people in their lives. When a person is lonely, often she puts people "at arm's length." To have a friend, a person needs to be open or friendly. When a person is not willing to have friendships, life is more difficult.

It is important for people to understand that love is for everyone, not just for certain people. Love is magnificent and wonderful.

People Who Love Children Inappropriately

People who love children in an inappropriate way are born with their chakra areas unusually intertwined. Instead of the chakras extending positively toward another person, the physical/red and sexually emotional/orange chakras intertwine like a twisted rope. The heart chakra is totally withdrawn, so that love and empathy are not a part of this person. This behavior satisfies merely a physical, sexual, and emotional need.

Why do people have this issue in their life? Is it from a past or a current lifetime?

Reincarnation has an effect. These children's souls choose this behavior before coming. Their parents had poor emotional or addictive health prior to copulating; therefore, their parents assisted in creating negative issues for their children. Their parents' poor health issues are the children's souls' choice to prepare for this behavior. Research could prove this true.

If it comes from a past life, the child who was abused in a previous life had very mixed feelings about the abuse. The child did not like being overpowered, so he needs power in this life. Secondly, he did not appreciate the physical act, but did receive some pleasure from it. This created the person's current need for overpowering a child for his own satisfaction.

A present-life situation can also create this behavior. When adults are sexually abusive to children, again, the children disliked the loss of power, but liked the feeling of sex. It is not something the child consciously understands. The power and sex become a need for him as he becomes an adult.

Does that mean abusers can't achieve sexual satisfaction with an adult?

In some cases, they can achieve satisfaction with both. In some cases, they cannot. Those who cannot are generally from a previous lifetime, whose emotions have carried over.

Why would a soul choose this?

The issue needs to be resolved for the soul to grow. It may take two or three lifetimes. Eventually, the person will understand the vulgarity, the power, and the hurting of this behavior. When the abuser understands this is part of the growth of the soul process, then it can be eliminated.

How?

It can be done a number of different ways. The best way is for them to learn to unconditionally love themselves, so then they can love others. Loving themselves allows them to release their anger and bitterness.

If it comes from a previous lifetime, how would they know what to release?

They know they have this need for power and satisfaction within them. Therapy may be needed. Past life regressions might also be used to assist in releasing this behavioral need. In either case, it is most important for the people to release and love themselves, so their soul can progress.

Reincarnation and the Connection between People

Reincarnation is real. As you say, "Why should I have only one lifetime? Why am I so lucky to be me, and not someone very unhappy and barely surviving?" Others may ask just the reverse of these valid questions.

You do have different lifetimes and lessons you must learn. For example, sharing can be on a survival level (food), a charity level (money or time), or an emotional level (understanding, compassion, or sympathy).

The lessons you learn from each lifetime go with you into your next lifetime. The information from each lifetime is added to the Akashic Record, an etheric book of the Hindu belief, chronicling your soul's actions. It holds the records of the souls with whom you have connected, your lessons, how you handled them, and all your thoughts and deeds.

The number of people you meet in each lifetime can be many, as in a card game of Solitaire, or a few, as in the game of Fish. The people in your present lifetime are most often people from a past life. Generally, you easily blend and work with these people. Some will bring you challenges, and from them you will learn the lessons for your soul's growth.

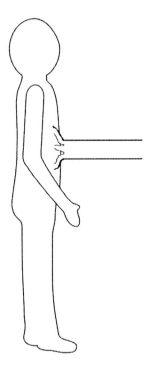

Figure 6 – Fearful Person's Chakra

Negative Power

The aura, love, and charisma all extend greatly from powerful people. When you recognize you have power, you can decide: "Will I use it to help people? or Will I use my power to control?" How and when you use power is a learning experience for you and others. People with power teach and are taught.

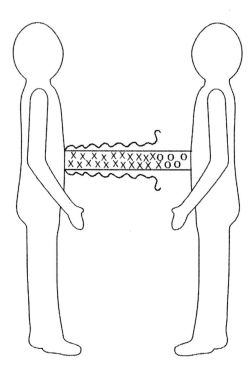

Figure 7 – Unequal Energy with Hooks

When a person is fearful, the chakras extend from a bigger root system. The size of the root system depends on the size of the fear **Figure 6**.

When the negative person's chakras become tentacles looking for people to control, they extend more than three-quarters of the way toward the root of a positive person to leech energy from the other person **Figure 7**. At that time, the self-confidence chakra of the positive person greatly recedes toward itself. This receding causes the person to feel badly about her ability to control her life. Eventually, the negative tentacles in a chemistry relationship hook into the positive person, so she loses all her self-confidence and becomes physically ill.

Rape

Coupling not done from choice is the violent sex of rape or subjugation. Rape is complete power dominance. The energy is not a gentle loving energy or even intense sexual energy but an act of violence. This violation, most often of the female, traumatizes the entire body—physically, emotionally, spiritually, and mentally.

Rape forces energy up through the chakras, even the spiritual chakra. In a violent rape, where the victim has not emotionally separated with an out-of-body experience, the victim finds it is especially difficult to recover. An out-of-body experience occurs when the conscious mind leaves the individual during various situations, both negative and positive, for protection or further work. For the individual who has traveled out of body during rape, the spiritual part has been saved. Although rape is a negative violation of the victim, it can be overcome.

Even though some rape victims become pregnant, many victims unconsciously create a chemical, emotional, and physical barrier to pregnancy.

Subjugation occurs when one partner controls the other. This type of sex is not out of choice. The partner is coerced into having sex. This coupling is different from the violence of a rape. Since the dominated person is not in agreement, her body sets up an emotional energy barrier in the sexual area.

Generally, people who participate in S and M, sadism and masochism, make a choice to participate. These are also negative experiences that require the body to emotionally feel inferiority or pain in order to feel satisfied. Although it is not positive, sometimes it is a necessary form of sex for some people.

What makes people want to participate in S and M?

Most of these people were abused and shamed as children. The only attention they received was when they were corporally punished. Sometimes children's minds will equate punishment with love.

Sometimes parents will even say, "I am doing this (physical punishment) because I love you." These children literally believe what their parents say. It becomes part of their belief system.

If they want to quit this practice, how do they do it?

For the person, the acceptability of S and M is very ingrained. To decide that this lifestyle is no longer of value, the person would need to make a conscious decision to leave. The biggest change requires the person to understand that love is a kind and gentle experience, not a painful one. Underlying the transformation requires a belief that God loves the person unconditionally, so they should love themselves unconditionally. Therapy would greatly help this person to find her self-love and release her need for pain.

Love and Forgiveness

Ideally, loving others unconditionally means totally accepting them, 100 percent. In reality, it means allowing other people to be who they need to be and to treat them with kindness, as you would expect to be treated. If someone creates problems for you, you must work through the issue within yourself.

Forgiveness is necessary for your soul's growth. When people forgive those who have hurt or murdered someone within their family, they have worked to release their anger or negative feelings, so they do not hold any grief within themselves. They have let go of their animosity. When they do not forgive, they carry their anger within themselves for a long time.

The Letter of Love

Once you decide it is not worth being in so much personal emotional pain and physical agony, letting go does not take a long time to accomplish. Forgiveness does not mean you lovingly embrace the other person. Forgiveness means that you let go of *your* feelings.

It is important for you to understand that, at times, love and life are terrific and great; at other times, you are challenged to remain loving. When you encounter people you do not understand, such as learning-disabled, blind, brain-damaged, homeless people, or even those of other cultures, and you do not know how to relate, you can still treat those people with kindness and respect. Your discomfort does not mean you should behave unlovingly.

What you should strive to do is to live the Golden Rule of the Christian faith, "Do unto others as you would have them do unto you," or any of the other interpretations of this by other religions, in every way, every day. When you try to be kind, it means you are "doing unto others." If you totally reject certain people, then you would not be living a loving life.

Most often, people try to accept other people, because they feel emotional connections. Even though acceptance is not a bond, it is a small connection. For example, if you are Caucasian, you have some understanding of Caucasians. The same is true if you are Black, Asian, Indian, etc.

Generally, similar people might not cause you discomfort or frighten you as much as the people from different cultures, countries, or nationalities.

This does not mean you are terrified of other types of people; it merely means you do not know or understand them. Therefore, you feel wary or confused because you might create an unintended problem or insult them. If you are open to other people, then you are being positive.

Occasionally, you may realize a person will not become a part of your circle of friends. Not accepting a person as a friend is saying, "I am not comfortable." Not accepting is okay as long as you are not negative about it. **When you negatively reject a person, it becomes exceedingly difficult for your soul to progress.**

Male, female, or coed groups often become exclusive and ridicule those who are not members of their clique. Ridiculing inhibits soul growth. **It is important to understand you must strive to accept all people as they are.**

25

Chapter Three

Orange Level Energy

Emotional feelings, interactions, sexuality, psychic, social interactions

Emotion

Mankind is on Earth to learn important lessons that on the other side are difficult to learn. Even though you believe a lifetime of 70 or 80 years is long, it is minute compared to the millennia some lessons take to learn on the other side. Yes, souls go to other planets to learn. **The Earth is a definitive learning experience, because it is all about emotion.**

Emotion is part heart and part brain and is vital to the human process. If there were no emotional links, the body, mind, and emotions of the heart would be separate and distinct.

Emotions are ruled by power. When you have power, you need to determine how to use it. Do you use your emotional power when you are angry, to hurt someone? Do you maintain a balance within yourself when angry? Or, do you use your emotional power to help people, because you have goodness in your heart? **Power is motivated by emotion.**

The Letter of Love

Some souls choose more difficult lifetimes so they can learn quickly. Others are overwhelmed by life and choose not to stand up for, take care of, or assert themselves. Some people do not protect themselves from danger or hurt; they may run away or divorce instead of attempting to deal with issues. If they leave, they will have to live another lifetime with the same issues.

Divorce is acceptable when one partner is unwilling to work at the relationship or when one partner tries to negatively control the other. When you lose your power, it is important to leave for your own self-worth.

Some people have many purposes, while others have a sole purpose. Some people raise children, work, volunteer, donate generously, and become famous. They have a whole variety of purposes in their lifetimes. Other individuals have a limited scope for this lifetime. **The reason people are here on Earth is to learn to handle their emotions and to unconditionally love both themselves and others, so their souls can progress.**

When a person has the courage to leave a negative relationship and then is killed, she has accomplished her life's goal. Even though others will miss her on the Earth plane, her soul has progressed. **It is most important for a person to love herself enough to take care of herself. If** she had left before the negative person's tentacles invaded her chakras, the death would not have occurred.

People who murder are obsessed with an individual. They are also engaged in a learning process. Once they realize that obsession is negative, they must learn how to eliminate their obsession.

When people commit crimes and are sentenced to jail, they create a difficult lesson for themselves. They will remain angry, until they release their obsession. If they truly change, they could be released from jail to lead a productive life.

The Chemical Reaction

Love is a chemical reaction between people that causes the physical attraction. Your heart expands the greatest amount in a romantic relationship. The second largest degree of expansion is with your children. If, as a child, you did not make strong family connections, neither your chakras nor chemical links form properly. A chemical reaction also exists between friends. Although the expansion is not as large as in a romantic relationship, being with a good friend causes your heart to dilate chemically and physically.

Unless there is some reason for you to become involved, generally you do not have chemical connections with other people. You only create chemical reactions with certain people: just with the family members you love, your adopted or biological children, and very good friends.

Rubber Bands

It is important to understand that channels of communication between people must remain open. Lack of communication causes relationship problems. In a loving relationship between two people, it is as though they have a strong rubber band of energy around their shoulders **Figure 8**. Love is blind, not just romantically, but also to the intensity of the real emotional connection between two people.

When a person says she is in love, and then says she is no longer in love, sometimes the news may come as a big surprise to her partner. If emotional love and communication were open and connected, this would not have happened. The emotional connection is necessary in love relationships.

When the relationship is strained or stressed, the rubber band is stretched thin. When a negative incident happens in the relationship, emotions can completely disconnect. Something must change to turn the situation around. Your friend Millie experienced a significant emotional separation from her husband. You asked her,

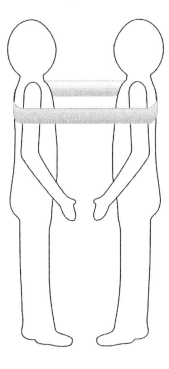

Figure 8 – Rubber Band Connecting Lovers

"What is the issue? How has he changed?" She answered that he had not changed. She asked, "You mean I have changed?" When she realized she had changed, her awareness made an important difference between them. Her attitude had prohibited her from being close, so she worked to eliminate her emotional barriers and reconnect to her husband.

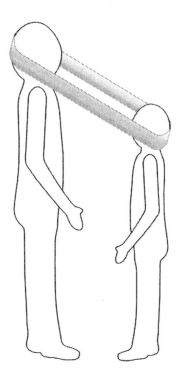

Figure 9 – Rubber Band Connecting Parent to Child

The process of emotional separation is not surprising. Upsetting events happen in relationships. These problems cause a person to emotionally separate from her partner. If the event is merely the size of a brick, often, all that is needed is self-realization. More often, little bricks build a wall so high a person feels that she cannot overcome it. Sometimes an event is the size of a boulder, which is much more difficult to overcome.

The emotional connection of children to their parents is not like the thick elastic band of energy, as it is between adults in loving relationships. The energy band connects the back of the head of the parent to the back of the head of the child **Figure 9**. The band expands and contracts as the child grows.

When a child is ready to separate, the elastic band loosens and spreads wide. When a parent talks to the child, the band reconnects. It is never entirely broken, unless there is an incident that causes a child to separate emotionally from her parent, such as in a sexually abusive situation.

There are so many connections – chemical, auric, bands, and chakras. Which is the most important connection?

Are all these connections necessary and real? They are very real. A person feels many different connections. When all occur simultaneously, true love is created.

The Emotional Connection between Children and Parents

Emotional relationships must be strong between parents and their children. Even though children do not like to be disciplined, it is important for them to learn society's rules, not just morals and ethics but also mores, so they can succeed.

The Letter of Love

There are societal rules that create problems for people, because these rules are contrary to their best interests. *For example, let's say in your neighborhood, receiving good grades in school is frowned upon. Your choice is to play the game to be a part of the group or to continue to achieve.* Therefore, **it is important for people to learn to evaluate rules, so they become the people they need to become for their soul's personal growth.**

Emotional love connections assist in creating chakra connections. Without the emotional connections between children and their parents, children will merely have a physical identity. These children will grow and function but will only experience their own pain. Because connected feelings are not a part of their personal makeup, they will not understand the possibility of relationship connections.

When children love their mothers, fathers, or initial caretakers, they have chakra connections as well as emotional, chemical reactions. As young men move through puberty, it is important for them to separate from their parents, especially their mothers. The chemical bond is strong, and it needs to diminish. For example, turning off a stream of water from a faucet is easily done. When the bond is too strong, it is like water pouring from a fire hose. Decreasing this strong bond is more difficult.

Disconnection from people creates more trauma and difficult challenges for a person in this lifetime. When there is a weak bond or rejection of the parent, the emotional connection link is nonexistent. This situation is very sad. It is important for children to have good partnerships with their parents, so as adults, they will have future healthy relationships.

When a parent dies, children have great difficulty adjusting. They will continue to extend a chemical connection to the deceased parent. Eventually, the bonds begin to retreat toward the body and almost curl inward. Sometimes they fold completely into themselves. This situation is unfortunate. Since parental love is the first type of love children experience, these children often have difficulty uniting chemically to their own children or to a partner in a relationship. As adults, if they realize their issue, they can make a conscious decision to work at healing themselves.

A chemical reaction begins with the permanent caregiver for the adopted child. If the natural parents immediately give up a child for adoption, the child does not connect with its biological parents. If the foster parents work with a child, they begin a small connection. The parents who adopt a young infant have the strongest connection. Chemically, the connection is brought out by the physical closeness, the emotional closeness, and the audible cooing to the baby. "Come on now, it's time to get up. You are so beautiful. It's time to eat."

The love between older children and their parents can be wondrous. If their parents have been caring, even though children leave home and form love and work relationships, the children will maintain less of a total heart connection link to their parents. A chemical connection remains, but to be independent, there must be a severing with the parents. The older children's tie to their parents becomes more intuitive. For example, when a child forms a life outside her parents, she must evaluate decisions based on what her parents taught her as well as her own evolving values.

Homosexuality

The emotional rubber band of love connects men to women, men to men, and women to women. Two males bond initially, because they have a physical attraction. In men, it is the physical first, then they get to know each other. Homosexuals learn from their chakra connections and life lessons.

Most of the time, two females bond because they have a relationship that causes them to be attracted. Women need the heart and intuitive chakras bonded, then they can become physical. Men are not necessarily seen as negative to these women, but men do not create a comfortable bond in their base chakra areas. This is neither right nor wrong.

When the soul reincarnates, as part of the birth process, the soul does not commit to a preference of being either male or female. This is partly karmic and partly caused by chemistry. Early on, the soul needs to make a commitment. The soul for homosexuals does not commit until later.

Why?

To make the choice of living differently than the norm is a decision that the soul may evaluate until the person is several months of age. The decision made is based on several factors. One, is the life I have chosen with these parents manageable?

You are actually given a choice?

Oh yes, an infant is given a choice of whether to stay with the family within the first few weeks or not.

Is this the reason for Sudden Infant Death Syndrome (SIDS)?

Yes. This does not mean the parents have done anything wrong. It merely means the parents were not whom the soul needed to assist it in its growth for this lifetime.

But, Sudden Infant Death Syndrome causes parents so much guilt.

That is part of the parents' soul lesson, because they have chosen loss as part of this life's learning. The loss does not have to be through SIDS; it could be through miscarriage or abortion.

Is there another reason for the soul to delay in making a decision of sexual preference?

The soul can realize the growth chosen was more than it intended. Therefore, the soul decides to make a traditional preference.

Is there a third reason?

Yes, the body chemistry is influenced by the predisposition of the parents at the time of copulation. Ambivalence of the parents about their own personal sexuality at the time of copulation can influence the chemical makeup of the child's soul.

Are you saying that parents can affect their child's sexual preference?

Yes and No. The parents, prior to manifesting as humans, have chosen the issue of homosexuality as part of their life's path. Also, parents-to-be need to understand their sexuality before they allow themselves to copulate for reproductive purposes.

The soul still has the right to decide its preference. If the soul decides against staying, the parents may have to address homosexuality in another way during this lifetime.

Homosexuality is a chakra issue, but it is also a soul decision. Homosexuality is neither bad nor good. **God does not judge homosexuals. God just sees souls on a path.** The soul has chosen this path because of the lessons it needs to learn in this lifetime.

The soul might have persecuted homosexuals in a previous life. This time, it may need to understand persecution and learn it is best for the soul to accept it without fear. If the soul can understand persecution in this lifetime, then the soul can advance further.

In Biblical times, there were various types of orgies, sexual free-for-alls. Orgies are not in the soul's best interest. Commitment of a man to a woman, man to a man, or woman to a woman is best. **God does not judge. God sees partnership as part of one's life progression. How you** *treat* **a partner is most important.**

If you treat your partner with disdain, cruelty, or meanness and not with love, this is how you are seen and judged at death. God does not judge you. You are only judged by yourself in your life review, a moving picture-like review of your entire life that includes all thoughts, words, and deeds.

How you treat others is added to your soul book, or the Akashic Record. All your actions will affect challenges for another lifetime. **As humans you have enough**

challenges. Do not create more challenges for yourself for future lifetimes.

Friendship

Friendship is more of an intellectual and chemical chakra reaction than a heart bond. A little heart chemistry is involved; otherwise, there would be no connection.

Linda, you met many people on your trips. Yet, you kept in touch with only one person. There is a reason for this, and it is chemical. You have a need to be with people who are open and honest. You do not have many friends because the honesty requirement limits you.

When people open their intuition, they instinctively know honest people from those who are playing games or are being difficult. They are able to discern honesty and sincerity.

Some people bond with many people, because they are so open. A person like your mother has a big connection to lots of people, because she is open to everybody. She does not have your honesty issue, yet people generally are honest with her.

You kept a strong connection with her for a long time. It was important that you severed your chemical dependence upon her. Now you are able to have a friendly relationship.

Orange Level Energy

You have a friend, Michael, who has a love connection with his wife but has few other people in his life. As a child, he was emotionally injured; therefore, his chakras withdrew. Some depression plays into his actions, but not much. His behavior is influenced by his personality.

When he and his wife were dating, she heard about his lack of connection from his few friends. At that time, she also did not have many friends, so she did not see it as a problem. Now she wants and needs friends. She has opened her love connection, but he still has not.

Since Cassie, his wife, moved frequently, her self-esteem was emotionally injured. Moving can be both a broadening and yet difficult experience. It is broadening, because the world is seen from an expanded viewpoint; it is difficult, because you must learn to make friends in the new area. Moving slightly injures the energy centers, because you must diminish in various degrees the relationships with your old friends and make new ones.

Friends allow each other to be individuals, and they are honest with each other. When friends give unsolicited advice, it may jeopardize the relationship. With a new acquaintance, the person giving unsolicited advice must be especially careful. You may still choose to give it, but do so very carefully.

The Letter of Love

When you learn to love and accept one another as friends, there may be issues you need to discuss. When this happens, you can discuss these issues positively, so your souls progress. When problems create a separation, your souls will not progress.

For example, if someone were having an affair, would the spouse want to be informed? This is an important question. The answer is not yes, everyone should know. The answer is, you need to find out what your friend would want to know. Then you can decide whether or not to tell her about the affair.

You might use a hypothetical situation to explore your friend's opinion. In conversation you might ask, "If you were this person, would you want to know?" Allow her to think about this question for a time, so the answer is a sound decision, not a hasty reaction. Then you would have some idea of what to say. You can use this technique in all areas of friendship.

Friends give each other moral support. You must understand that your preferences may not be the same as someone else's. Linda, you learned this lesson through your friend Marsha. She did not want anyone to accompany her when she traveled a great distance to visit doctors. This was difficult for you to accept, since you would like having a friend along with you if the situation were reversed. What she wanted was right for her.

When your friends have issues, you are available to help them. For example, to your friend Sally, you and another person said, "Why don't you love yourself enough to take care of yourself?" Now, she is taking better care of herself, because she needed to hear it. Part of her healing had to do with the loss of her son. She had to love herself despite what she regarded as mistakes on her part.

A mistake is never what happens; it is how one perceives what happens. If one perceives something as a mistake, then it is a mistake. It is only a mistake for that person. It may not be a mistake in a different situation or for a different person.

Your friend Katherine is a strong, direct personality. You are one of the few people who can get along with her. Both of you are honest, but you are gentler. She has broken relationships because of her directness and honesty. Because of her idea of truth, friendship is difficult for some of her friends, but you accept her directness. She does not pursue some issues with you, because she respects and understands you.

She is a capable person and is doing exactly what she needs to do to help herself. She will progress as a soul in many ways in the next year and a half, because she will heal herself. You must understand that what you do for her is important; what she does for herself and for you is equally important.

Togetherness

When coworkers work positively on a project, a relationship can form, which may cause them to feel a romantic connection. They think, "I like this person. This person is doing a good job. I think things will work out." A small chemical connection is built. At first, the connection is not necessarily romantic. If one person is not in a current romantic relationship or feels that his relationship at home is weak, their bond can turn romantic. **When a platonic relationship turns romantic on one side, the relationship becomes unequal.**

When the now romantically bonded person reveals her feeling for the platonically bonded person, he may be surprised, because he was unaware that her emotional center changed.

When two people work and play together, they connect dramatically. Yet, whether they are together or apart, each must have the freedom to develop separately. Being apart gives you time to develop, regenerate, and revive.

Orange Level Energy

When you are with a group of people, whether you interact or not, you may be drained by their energy. People drained by coworkers need to be alone to sleep or recharge to remain healthy. Even a different personality, like someone very soothing, can assist in re-energizing some people.

People who leave work terribly exhausted need to protect themselves on their jobs so they feel safe and not energetically drained. Visualizing a bubble, an envelope, a box, or any other container to put themselves and their aura inside before stressful interactions can be helpful in retaining their energy, so they can interact with the people and their messages.

Their solar plexus should be protected before interacting with others in a one-on-one situation. They can put an object—their arm, a purse, a map, papers, or even a briefcase—over their solar plexus to assist them in retaining their energy. For example, sometimes your friend Leland goes fishing by himself after work. On his return, he feels regenerated. There were no human beings to drain his energy.

Sleeping with, separating from, or being with someone you love and care about also recharges your body, because energy is not being pulled from your chakras or aura.

Occasionally, we need to be around other people to be revived. For your friend Lydia, friends are an energy input and a change of scene.

In a true-love relationship, whether you are together or apart, you help each other grow. To be stuck in a controlling relationship, where the other person is taking away your energy, is constantly exhausting. You become powerless. This is what happened to Velma. She grew powerless, because her energy was totally drained. Since her spouse controlled her, she had no way of recharging. It was a difficult relationship for her to end.

Sometimes the person who is being controlled must die to break away from the relationship. Occasionally, friends give moral support to the controlled person. Often, when that person finally realizes she has lost her power, she will gather her courage to leave. For her soul's growth, she must leave to regain her personal power.

There are people, who, after losing their power with coworkers, stay in these situations. Even though the situation drains their physical strength and their self-confidence, they remain for other reasons. It is most important for them to leave, sooner rather than later, to maintain their strength and sense of worth.

Some people put this off for a long time and become physically ill. The illness will be a life-changing traumatic one, not just a minor irritation. Then the major illness gives them a reason to leave.

Relationships between friends are important. Even though people do not see each other for months or years, often it feels as if they never quit their conversation. This is because of a strong karmic connection. This bond is as crucial as the emotional and physical connection and is very powerful.

Linda, you have a friend or two with whom you have a strong karmic connection from a past life. You have something to teach them, and they have something to teach you. They will move on, and so will you, but you will remain friends in a special way. How you interact with other people is of primary importance.

Lack of Sleep and the Chakras

During the day, your chakra energy centers project unequally. When you sleep, they adjust themselves by becoming relaxed and returning to balance. Your crown and third-eye chakras are extremely active at night. At times, you retain issues in your body, because you are not ready to release them to the Akashic Record, the soul library where your present life is recorded. Your reluctance to let go of information is what awakens you.

47

When you cannot sleep in the middle of the night, use your mind to distract yourself. Write down your thoughts, make a list, or make a game plan for the issues bothering you. Writing thoughts on paper releases the information running around in your mind, so you can return to sleep. Once you are calm and asleep again, your body then permits the intuitive and spiritual chakras to do their work in the Akashic Record.

Physical discomforts will also disturb your sleep. When you are ill or in pain, your chakras become tense and imbalanced. They try to readjust themselves by slowing down and receding, which causes your body to become disturbed and awake. While position changes may be helpful, a thorough investigation into the emotional connection of body issues may be needed. Those with long-term karmic issues may suffer more.

When you awaken in the middle of the night, Linda, you hear the songs you are rehearsing in your head. You have asked not to hear as much music, so we have cut it back for you. You hear music only occasionally now.

Illness

Some people say that illness is strictly something we create for ourselves. Sometimes, this is true. Illness is created because we have internalized our thoughts and emotions. We have not loved ourselves enough to positively talk to ourselves and with other people. Some people's illnesses are a form of retribution or punishment for malicious acts they have done to others. People need to understand this is how life works.

So do people manifest illness as karmic payback, because they were malicious?

Sometimes. The illness would not necessarily have manifested if the person had not been malicious. Not all illness is due to malice. Sometimes illnesses are used by souls so they will understand ridicule and non-acceptance. Some illnesses are also a choice of the soul to learn lessons of restriction—coping with prolonged pain, learning to make wise decisions, learning to become independent of a family, learning to become a part of a community at large, accepting dependence, etc.

Genetic disabilities are carried from generation to generation from both the imprinted egg and sperm. Scientific advances have helped many more children survive. Children born prematurely often have dysfunctions and are subjected to medical procedures, which also can create additional disabilities.

Does having a disabled child mean parents should love the child less?

No.

Does it mean they should love this child more?

No. What it means is, this child comes with many issues. The parents' souls have agreed to assist the child, so all their souls can grow, which is why the child was born to them in the first place.

Many chemicals in society adversely affect babies and children. Some of the mother's blood goes through the umbilical cord to feed the fetus until it is ready to leave the womb; therefore, it is wise that the government and doctors recommend that pregnant women do not use chemicals, because they can cause harm during the pregnancy.

Feelings and Depression

When we are emotionally stuck, we cannot see any "light at the end of the tunnel." We see only darkness and become depressed. Most people have had periods of depression in their lives. Few people have not been touched by sadness, even if only for a day, a week, or several months. When people deny their depression, it can become prolonged. It can go on for years. If they are deeply depressed, their depression turns into mental illness. This does not mean they are "bad." It means subconsciously, they have chosen not to be part of a particular situation.

The depression from mental illness does not relate to bipolar or manic depressive disorders, which are imbalances of the physical body. Souls have chosen these illnesses during this lifetime, so they can progress. *At this point, I was requested to give examples of three people I know who released their emotional depressions in positive ways.*

I know a woman who married a controlling husband. Often, she tried to stand up for herself but found that his energy was much stronger than hers. Because she felt it was wrong to leave any marriage, she stayed and grew depressed. It amazed me, because this was her second marriage to a controlling husband. After a number of years, the second husband died. Several years later, she married another controlling husband. Only during this third marriage was she able to stand up for herself.

Second, I know a man who was unhappy at work, because his industry had changed to make his position less effective. He was determined to stay in his job in order to receive his retirement benefits. After several years, he retired early with his benefits. He soon found another position, where he was valued by others in his workplace. Only then was he fully able to release his depression.

Third, I know two women who moved to different communities. In each case, they tried to make friends but found connections limited. Both women yearned for the friendships of their past. Eventually, they became depressed. After a while, one went to a counselor, was put on medication, and came out of her depression. Finally, she found friends and activities in town. The second woman tried to remain active but continually fought depression, which decreased after finding a job and making new friends.

Love and Nature

Many people have good relationships with animals. **Some people connect even more to animals than to people.** Unlike people, animals give unconditional acceptance. In general, domestic animals give unconditional love to humans through their heart and spiritual chakras.

When you treat animals with love, they return love in abundance. Your animals, Linda, are loving, because you love them. Even though at times you do not understand them, there are also times they do not understand you.

Most people should have animals around, because a human needs to experience unconditional love. Adults love animals with their hands. They do not necessarily need to have them in their laps to connect to their chakras. Animals easily relate and assist in emotionally or physically healing people. They connect to patients by giving them emotional rest they need to feel less anxious about themselves and their illness.

Orange Level Energy

If animals were allowed a longer time with patients, they would heal more quickly. Pets should not be in hospitals 24 hours a day, because they would be too burdensome on the staff. Pets benefit patients greatly in nursing-home situations with their unconditional love.

Animals are important in assisting the healing of children and adults. The chakra connections between children and animals are strong. Often, children connect to animals with their whole bodies. They want to touch animals with their chests, arms, legs, and heads. Animals reduce the fear of hospitalization. They can be held and will love back. If children could, they would have animals in bed with them.

Only when something occurs that scares children do they become afraid of animals. Your fear of snakes, Linda, is now being corrected. *Let me explain. One day when I was age 5 or 6, as I walked in a small orchard, a small snake slithering in the grass scared me. Until a few years ago, I could not even look at a picture of a snake.*

When you eliminate fear from your body, Linda, you will eliminate your fear of snakes. You choose not to go into the snake house at the zoo. You could have handled looking at the snakes. After all, you did look at the resting python and boa constrictor in the other part of the zoo.

The Letter of Love

Generally, domestic animals continue to extend unconditional love until a person does something to alienate the animal. Continuous negative treatment of animals can turn them fearful or vicious. The person who shows love and understanding becomes close to her animals.

Dogs love unconditionally because their auric energies are easily compatible with people. Their chakra connections are not as strong. Their chakra bonds are with the people they love the most and are closest to. If something happens to the people dogs love, the chakra tie detaches and creates a wound that takes time to heal. Dogs can then reconnect with other people, but not in the 100 percent unconditionally loving and bonding way the animal had with the original owner.

Cats are different. They have conditional love. If you accept who they are, then cats are willing to be in the family. They never totally connect with their chakras. When cats bond closely with their owners, they just have auric connections. Linda, you had a very loving cat, Snagglepuss. Yet, he had only auric connections with you.

Fish do not have chakra or auric connections; they just are. Birds may have auric connections if they are close, but often they do not become close.

Horses can form close bonds with their owners. A person's root chakra connects more directly to the horse's chakras. When the relationship is good, horses create close connections to those who take care of them. Horses feel the connections and know how people treat them. Horses that have been mistreated also feel negative connections. They can buck, be rude, and become destructive.

Other farm animals can connect. Generally, farmers detach emotionally from their animals, because they know the animals will be used for other purposes, such as food and hides.

When children take care of 4-H animals, they become closely connected. They make an auric connection. Usually, these children learn to disconnect from their animals before they are sold.

Some people connect more to animals than to people because of a traumatic childhood. Even wild birds visiting the immediate area near a home can feel the love that radiates from a person who is open to animals.

Past lifetimes may influence a person's feelings for animals. Sometimes issues are important for the person to carry from one lifetime to another so they can be resolved.

For example, did my fear of snakes just come from this lifetime or did I always have it? I can never remember a time when I was able to look at a picture of any reptile, whether in black and white or color.

The love of nature requires compatibility between the aura of the person to that of plants or animals. This mutual connection is beautiful. It cannot be negative love. Yes, Nature provides horrific experiences periodically but not because an individual must learn a lesson. Rather, lessons of compassion and understanding need to be learned in the various parts of the world where natural calamities occur. When there are tornadoes, droughts, hurricanes, and famines, compassion is the lesson.

I have heard that people in an area can be so negative that they attract tornadoes, etc. Is this true?

Certain areas of the world are prone to disasters where storms habitually occur. They can be charted. When people build up negative energy near one of these areas, a storm will veer in that direction. The storm was not initially attracted to that place; it was redirected.

What about people who take advantage of disasters for monetary profit?

Some people's lessons are twofold. One, there are compassionate people; but also, there are those who take advantage of situations. *For example, after a hurricane several years ago, people sent lumber to the area. Some providers sold it at elevated prices taking advantage of the residents.* Some people have double lessons to learn.

Earthquakes are a natural process of the Earth's energy trying to adjust itself. Linda, you have noticed that earthquakes in one part of the world create earthquakes in another part. This is a balancing system. Love is shown by the compassion extended to people affected by earthquakes.

Some people think that those who live in an area where Nature creates recurring devastation, should leave the area. They should. But, some learn slowly or do not learn at all. Some people are unwilling to leave their homes, the beauty of the oceans, or other places where hurricanes, typhoons, and tidal waves occur.

Islanders who live in villages close to the water occasionally experience tidal waves, which are the result of underwater earthquakes. Formerly, some cultures saw natural calamities as an expression of God's anger. In fact, Nature is merely rebalancing. Unfortunately, these people are in the path.

Nature is not making a conscious decision to destroy, so that others will show compassion. All natural disasters are a matter of cause and effect. Tidal waves are one way for islanders to learn profound lessons of death, lack of power, compassion, persistence, planning, cooperation, etc.

Astrology and Your Life

Astrology is important guidance for your life, because you are affected by the energy of the universe. The planets are a way of describing this energy, as is numerology, the energy of the numbers of your birth date and your given name. Astrology is an interpretation of how universal energy affects you.

People who discredit astrology are often rejecting the brief generalities found in newspapers. A full astrological reading describes exactly who you are in this lifetime. Astrology is important knowledge that can assist you in understanding yourself and in preparing for challenges.

If challenges are addressed now, you will not have to deal with them in the next lifetime. Have an astrological reading from time to time to see what the energies are bringing. With this knowledge, you may know who you are so you can positively be prepared to address potential future challenges.

Chapter Four

Yellow Level Energy

Intellect, thinking, planning, linear thinking

Predestination versus Free Will

There is a difference between predestination and free will. Predestination is the outline of all the different issues you will encounter during your lifetime. If you are predestined to have issues in a certain area, you will definitely have them. Free will is how you handle these challenges. How you work through a problem is strictly how you choose to deal with it. You may or may not deal with the problems as easily as others or you may deal with problems better on one day than another. Previous lifetimes influence what you need to work on during your current lifetime.

People choose their personalities before coming to Earth. How they react to their challenges is based on their chosen personality. Some personalities move a person forward; other personalities hold people back, until they are ready to move forward. Some personalities are totally overwhelmed by life and locked in place. It is important for people to understand their unique personalities, so they can make conscious decisions for their soul's growth.

Being human gives you choices or options. You can choose either the positive or the negative. **Choices that move you closer to God and unconditional love are ones that move your soul farther along the path.** The choices you make that create problems for you take you farther away from the path of unconditional love. *For example, if you tell a lie, you will have to continue to tell lies to cover up your initial untruth to keep from being caught. If you cheat someone, you can either ignore it or make restitution and move yourself back toward the path of unconditional love.*

If you choose the negative, you prohibit or slow down your soul's growth. The beautiful part of being human is that you can always make a change in direction toward unconditional love of yourself and others. When you return to the true path, whether you call it finding salvation, finding God, or being a good person, you eliminate many problems for your soul in another lifetime. If a person stays off the path her entire lifetime, her soul will have to deal with the same issues in greater magnitude in the next lifetime.

The universe challenges you three times to figure out how to manage a problem. If you manage it well the first time the problem arises, you will not have problems the second and third time the problem occurs. If you do not manage it well the first time, the second and third time you will have even greater problems.

For example, a family has to decide whether or not to invite a family member to an occasion. They say, "We do not like this person, so we will not invite her." In your heart, you feel that she should be invited. You might say, "I disagree with this decision. I believe she should be invited. She is a member of the family. Not having her here will create a problem." This can make a transition into the discussion.

If you do not say anything the first time, the second time the discussion happens, you will be more frustrated. The family member's alienation has already occurred, and the family believes they are in "the right." They will feel less guilty about not inviting her a second time.

If you had spoken up the first time, and the second time the family makes the same choice, they will say, "so and so disagrees, but we will do it anyway." The decision may be easier, but the family may still feel some guilt. If you speak up each time, or have at least spoken once, they will realize this is an issue for you.

If the third time they decide not to invite her, and you have not expressed your opinion, you may become angry. When you do, you may say something to alienate yourself from the family and divide the family further.

All family interactions are a part of every person's soul work. The people you have in your life for a long time can create various issues because of your past life connections.

Are there cases when the family should not invite a member?

Yes. If someone is being purposely destructive to a family, the situation is different from a person who is just being an irritation. This is different from, "Aunt Jody drives me nuts." If someone is purposely destructive and causing chaos, then the family can make a decision to exclude her by standing up for itself.

If the destructive person continues to be invited, the family has not acted as a cohesive unit; they are being manipulated by her. This destructive person is in the family, so both the family group and each member can learn. The family needs to detach from that person, not just exist with the chaos on a long-term basis. The family must separate from her.

This relationship is also a lesson for the destructive person. A manipulative person must be separated from the family, so she will realize that they will not be manipulated or destroyed any longer. Then the person has the option of changing her behavior.

Linda, you did something similar with Geneva, who had acted unacceptably for years and who was causing chaos for you. It was necessary for you to stand up to her, so she could learn that her behavior was not acceptable. You are one of the few people to make her look at herself. People say she is too old to change. **No one is ever too old to change.** True, she may not change, but you made her aware of how she behaves.

We must learn when to connect to people and when to disconnect. When others create havoc or negativity in our lives, it is important to separate from them. People always have an opportunity to change their way of behaving throughout their lives. Not all humans improve their behavior before they die. If they don't, they must go through another cycle of being the type of people they were. Most humans do change or improve, so they can move past many of this lifetime's challenges. Some people do not understand this until the very last minute of their lives.

The people you meet and issues you face are challenges created for each lifetime. The incidents that happen repeatedly are the lessons for this lifetime. This is how your soul learns.

Decision Making

The love of a parent for an infant is all-consuming. As infants age, it is important for children to make small decisions, so they know how to make bigger decisions later. If they have not been allowed to make minor decisions from the time they were young, children will become frustrated in making major decisions in their lives and make bad choices.

Decision-making should increase as a child ages. You create choices for a child when you say, "Would you like cereal or eggs?" More judgment is required when you say, "Would you like clothes this style or that style?" Suppose you tell the child, "Choose between a bicycle or a computer." This creates a big dilemma, which requires her to weigh the options. Whatever the child decides, she must be willing to abide by her selection. When the child makes a choice she regrets, it means she is learning an important lesson. In the future, she can use her knowledge of this situation to make wiser decisions.

Later, she can make big decisions, such as, "Do I want to go out with this person? Do I want a relationship or friendship? Do I want a sexual relationship with this person? Do I want to be married to him? Do I want children?" These are major life decisions.

People must learn to relate in a loving way, by allowing each other to be who they need to be, without control. Often, loving someone is difficult, because your agendas are different. Therefore, you need to understand that people are in relationships to learn how to be themselves.

This does not mean that compromises are not possible. They are very possible. A problem is solved by deciding what is right for each of you. Sometimes, because the other person wants to do something and you love him, you go along or find a middle ground. When you love, compromise is a way of life.

Even though you do things together, you must allow the other person to explore his interests in his own time and space. Doing so improves the quality of the time spent together.

It is important for people to understand that **the purpose of humanity and humanness is to learn to love. Unconditional love is the way to reach this goal**. It is difficult to achieve, because your parents, your upbringing, and other factors of your youth have influenced you. To accept people for themselves is as close as most people can come to unconditional love.

The Golden Rule of the Christian faith, "Do unto others as you would have them do unto you," or any of the other religion's interpretations of this rule, is a way of being unconditional. Unconditional love means accepting people for who they are, even though they may be angry. **Loving**

people do not persecute people for their beliefs. Love does not mean you have to agree with everybody.

Unconditional love is accepting people without judgment. When you unconditionally love, you see people as souls, not as a product of their actions. You must understand that some people have issues that cause them to behave poorly. What you say to yourself is, "This is a person who has some kind of issue. I do not know what it is. Their anger does not make them a bad person; it just makes them an angry person." This is similar to loving the child but not her behavior. Do you see the difference between the two? So it is very important that you look at each person with acceptance.

Being judgmental is negative. Humans find it difficult to stop judging, because it becomes automatic. You have been taught to make judgments and decide right from wrong based on specific criteria. You are not taught to evaluate people as people. There is a difference between judging and evaluation.

If a person seems to have unlimited joy, then many say, "This person must be wonderful." Living in joy does not make her any better than the angry person; the joy just makes her what she is.

Being able to accept unconditionally is critical. Each time you do, you move your soul's growth forward.

The Bible says, "Judge not that ye be not judged." Also, "Vengeance is mine saith the Lord." Killing is an emotional act. Sentencing a dangerous person to jail is different from being judgmental of everyone. Society needs to be protected from criminals. When you sit on a jury, you must evaluate the person from "the love of all mankind" viewpoint. You should evaluate each situation according to the facts. As you know, facts can be skewed one way or the other, but you must be able to conclude that the accused person has done inappropriate actions. Therefore, this person needs to be jailed for society's protection. You must evaluate the person in a just way.

Can you be an unconditionally loving person and vote for the death penalty?

It is important for you to understand that vengeance has been used for generations. The purpose of vengeance is to destroy another person. Even though the death penalty exists, it is not wise to use it. The death penalty is not a deterrent; it merely eliminates another mouth to feed in a prison.

If society had a no-parole policy for hardened criminals, they would never be released. Some people often comment, "We are housing many dangerous prisoners, which is costing society a lot of money." This is true, but there is always a chance that a person can change.

The Letter of Love

The isolation on death row is excessive punishment. Yes, many on death row are violent criminals, but if they have truly transformed, they should be allowed to interact with other prisoners. Isolation is an unacceptable, inhumane punishment.

Even though prisons are negative societies, *if* prisoners are willing, love can be learned. Yes, it is difficult for prisoners to become loving, but it is possible. Prisons should separate those who are transforming for the better from the angry prisoners. Prisoners can learn to care, to interact positively, and even learn to love.

Prisoners who have a change of heart could be released. The prison guards, not necessarily the officials, should have input into the process. Their daily contact gives them knowledge of whose heart or attitude has really changed to become loving or forgiving. Guards also know which inmates have released their personal anger. You see, love is important to learn in all aspects of society. When transformed prisoners are released, they can become productive and positive people.

You saw the film *The Shawshank Redemption*, which showed a long-time prisoner who could not cope with society outside a prison. This can be the case. Some prisoners are only comfortable in a prison culture.

They know the rules and are uncomfortable with making decisions.

Positive and Negative Chakras

As we said, positive people extend their loving chakras equally toward other people. Negative or hateful people have tentacles that extend from their chakras to draw in others in every relationship.

Negative people's tentacles extend forward and then go backwards toward themselves. Their tentacles are actually wavering in the air, screaming and reaching for other people **Figure 10**. Negative people are disconnected from everyone. Their tentacles extend, like a tight fan, to form a protective wall in front of themselves to keep other people from hurting them. When negative people find vulnerable people, they draw them into their space. Usually, only a small number of people respond.

In the negative relationship, the negative partner extends chakra energy, like a hand grabbing the energy of the other person. **When one person feels overwhelmed by another, the negative person's emotional chakra has extended more than halfway toward the other person's chakra area.** The connection is no longer balanced, and major problems are created. Although the emotional center is the primary extending chakra, the other chakras to some

69

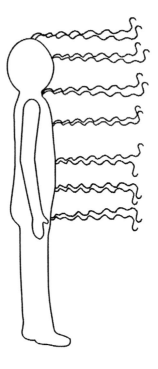

Figure 10 – Screaming Tentacles

degree are affected. The person having her energy taken away must separate from the negative partner, so she can grow and become the individual she needs to become for her soul to evolve.

Chakras and the Mentally Ill

Mental illness is not a conscious choice. It is an unconscious, freewill choice. It exists when people cannot handle their life issues. Their chakra energy diminishes to the point where they unconsciously choose mental illness. The chakras of mentally ill people are disconnected from reality. Sometimes, there are so many traumas to a patient's energy systems that their chakras disengage. Occasionally, the disconnection is physical. The disassociation is in the mental and spiritual areas most of the time.

Generally, they can be reconnected with the unconditional love of animals, as well as slowly working through the issues. A person must be willing to confront her problems. For reconnection to occur, small pieces of the chakras must return over time.

Is this what causes the need for a "soul retrieval"?

It is similar, but a soul retrieval is different. When people are mentally ill, they lose energy from their chakras. Their sense of self can be returned through aromatherapy, symbols, conversation, and incidents.

Soul retrieval, on the other hand, is the loss or shutdown of portions of the soul. This happens because life incidents have traumatized the soul's essence. The loss of soul essence is caused by other people negating an individual by rendering him invalid. Almost everyone has some loss of soul essence over a lifetime. Mental illness and soul loss may occur simultaneously or separately.

When people cannot speak, the throat chakra is also disengaged. If mentally ill people are unable to talk, therapists will find working with them difficult. Even though these patients do not respond, they hear what is being said. They just act as if they cannot respond, as a defense mechanism. They hear the same way people in a coma hear.

People who are mentally ill need a great deal of therapy. Often, these people are kept in a safe place and therapy is done for an hour, once or twice a week. Daily therapy would be better. Even those patients who do not talk absorb information.

Competent therapists do not just question patients unable to respond, but instead, they focus on issues, so the patient can think about healing. Then their chakras heal much faster. When patients cannot talk, the throat chakra may be the last place to heal. All counseling must be given with love and understanding.

Therapists can use sensory stimuli to assist patients to move more quickly along their path toward healing. Colors, aromas, and odors, both pleasant and unpleasant, may help patients reconnect to events from their lives they are trying to avoid. This is especially true for people who have amnesia.

Chapter Five

Green Level Energy

Family, love, children, balance, nurturing, inner connecting, mother, home

The Importance of Balance

You must learn to make distinctions and differentiate between various wise and unwise situations, so your life and soul move forward. **Rather than living your life controlled by your emotions, live confidently with God.** For God loves everyone and would like everyone to move their soul toward unconditional love. **Once a soul achieves total unconditional love, it does not reincarnate.**

Often people do not grow, because they are afraid of change. Remaining stagnant prevents their soul from progressing.

It is important to understand, Linda, that your purpose here is for personal growth and to assist others in moving their souls closer to unconditional love. Much of what we teach, Linda, you already know. Many of these messages are believable to you, but when you find an idea that is not credible to you, you do not accept it.

You had problems with the Rosicrucian beliefs. Rosicrucians are members of the fraternal order or brotherhood that teaches techniques to fully utilize their minds to achieve their wants and needs. Their followers believe a person should not vary in emotion. Living an emotionless life is difficult for you to understand, Linda.

Currently, you believe that emotions—joy, sadness, happiness, and depression—are a part of life. You believe they are part of the human experience, so you can find a personal emotional balance. Most people are not willing to give up emotional highs and lows. They like the highs, because they feel so good. They do not like the lows, but see lows as a part of life's growth process.

Rosicrucians have learned to balance the imbalances, so they do not have emotional highs and lows. If the balancing is done out of will versus understanding, it is improper. Balancing is only proper if it is totally understood. For example, this is a low time, and I can understand it; yet, I still feel composed about what is happening. This is a high time, and it's wonderful, but I feel totally balanced about what is happening.

The Rosicrucians have developed a means of balancing. Most Rosicrucians have learned through a long, definitive process to stabilize their emotional energies. Their way is not easy for the vast majority of people.

We all move forward at different paces. We need to understand and be grateful for our lessons. Each lesson learned moves our soul closer to unconditional love.

The illness you had a few years ago, Linda, would not have been as acute if your emotions had been balanced. Since you did not understand why you were ill, you felt the illness more keenly; therefore, it was difficult. When you understood that the illness was fear-based, you released your fears, so you could heal.

Love and the Heart

Romantic love is not only an emotional chakra feeling, it is also a chemical feeling. **When the heart feels the positive effects of love, it literally grows a fraction of an inch and glows magnificently.** You actually can feel it swell in your body. This type of love feels wonderful. Chemical feelings of romantic love can happen to all of us.

Chemical is different from chemistry. We are not talking about chemistry, that special, magnetic chakra and auric connection from a past life that people feel. We are talking about the chemical reaction of romantic love.

In a chemical connection of romantic love, the heart releases a chemical that creates a bond with the other person. With a chemical tie, you can fall quickly in and out of love. Your friend Gretchen feels romantic love with every male she meets and is sure that each man is "the one." She feels the chemical swelling in her body, so she believes she is in love.

When you are continually around your love, the chemical does not react as much as it did when you were in a romantic mood. Familiarity causes the chemical to decrease and the romantic love to diminish. When a person has been away from her love for a while, her heart swells with joy during reunion. The intensity of the chemical is affected by how the relationship is progressing.

During everyday life, the chemical recedes into the body and stays there until you meet again. When a person argues, the chemical definitely withdraws into each person's body. After a major argument it is more difficult for the chemical to release again.

The chemical does not extend itself 100 percent of the time but extends and retracts depending on the situation. It is only drawn out when you need it. It is important for the body to have this reaction, because to extend continually, the chemical would be physically too intense. It would exhaust the body. You need to have time away from the one you love to recharge and be yourself.

Romantic love creates a wonderfully deep connection. In true love, people are deeply bonded. They do things for one another out of love, not because the action is required.

Sometimes in a romantic or marriage relationship you have to do things for your partner you would rather not. When he is ill or in need of moral support, true love is making yourself available to your partner. You give your help, do not demoralize, or create problems for him.

Some people whose partners do not give moral support do the best they can in challenging situations, but they find it difficult. These partners only half love. Emotionally, they give only a small amount of themselves.

Childhood emotional issues affect how people love. Those who come from dysfunctional family backgrounds find it difficult to love others. When we love, we do not have "our defenses up." We cooperate smoothly in work, illness, and play.

People need to learn the importance of the love connection. Love is knowing and caring about another. We seek the other person's good most of the time, but not at the expense of ourselves. **Loving does not mean giving up who we are.**

Love presents facts given in an honest, not brutal, manner. When people have real love and affection for each other, facts can be stated in a positive way. Real affection has to do with caring for another emotionally and physically.

This is what is meant in the Christian marriage vows, "in sickness and in health, 'til death do you part." This phrase intends that the marriage should be a lifelong commitment. If one of the marriage partners is abusive or controlling and prohibits the other person from being the wondrous person she can be, then the abused partner must leave the marriage for her own soul's growth. She should not feel guilty for leaving. "'Til death do you part" should not create guilt.

The phrase "richer or poorer" means adjusting to life's trials. You support your partner in both good times and challenging times. In some cultures, marriage is based only on money. Such partnerships may or may not evolve into true love relationships.

It is also important to realize that we are here on Earth to learn lessons. One of our lessons is learning how to give moral support to others. Destroying or injuring another inhibits our soul growth. When we understand that our actions cause our partner additional pain, a change of our behavior is needed. For example, let's say your partner has a decision to make, one that has been unresolved for a couple of years. Although his indecision is causing problems for you, your spouse's indecision is acceptable. What is unacceptable is for you to say, "Let's do this or that." Over time, this causes your spouse emotional turmoil. Let him make his decision in his own time.

Waiting is difficult for the person impatient for a decision. To make it better for the person waiting, discuss the questions in "what if" scenarios. Discussion in this manner will help you deal emotionally with the indecision. Then your partner can make his decision in his own time. This will help your partner feel good about himself. **The purpose of loving another is to love someone with your best self for his best self.** Do not be selfish with your love.

You can love more than one person, because we love people in different ways. For example, you love two people deeply, which one should you marry? You must decide with your intuition, not with your logic. When you go with your logic, sometimes you pay a price. Your logic may assert, "I can do this." But if you are not emotionally joined, the relationship will not be supportive. **Humans need loving, supportive relationships.**

People who marry based on real love relationships are truly happy. Occasionally, we may love someone who is financially unsuccessful. This situation can create a problem for some people. The choice we make is not wrong, because no matter who we choose, we will grow from the relationship.

When husbands or wives have an affair or numerous affairs, negative relationships are created. **If one is in a true marriage relationship, you will be totally connected to your spouse; therefore, affairs are not acceptable.** People who have this need to play around create problems for everyone concerned — their partners, families, and friends.

The offended partner needs to ask, "Is this what I want in my life?" Some people are willing to say, "Yes, I will put up with the affair because of the money, the prestige, or the name I have in this relationship." In essence, they are selling out and emotionally destroying themselves. This attitude does not advance their soul's growth. Over time, someone staying in an unfaithful relationship will create a physical illness for herself. At that point, the emotionally hurt person must decide whether to continue in the relationship or leave.

Sometimes a partner is unaware of the infidelity or is in total denial. Knowing of an infidelity for many years also creates an illness unless you believe your partner has a right to play around. Even though this type of relationship is not ideal, it may work for some. A couple staying in a relationship that openly accepts infidelity is neither right nor wrong. It is just not typical.

Although a man-to-man or woman-to-woman relationship is also not typical, if it is a true monogamous relationship, it is very positive.

Child and Parent Love

Love is important for our personal experiences and growth. Love stimulates babies and children to thrive until they are grown. Love gives them self-confidence and their greatest joy. They know that no matter what happens their family loves them.

If the love connection is broken, sadly, these children have to deal differently with the issues of who they are and how to relate to other people. If these children have not learned to relate, then it is difficult for them to bond with others.

This is the case for many children who do not have both parents. When any parent is too busy to take the time to truly connect, children do not learn how to love. Their friends find them difficult to be around. Neglected children have neither the love nor the physical and the emotional support they need. This lack affects their future unions.

Many children grow up afraid of commitment and love. Even if parents are involved in activities outside the home, children need love, hugs, friendly touching, and conversation: "I will fight for you because I love you; I will take care of you." These statements make children feel protected and loved.

Lack of loving attention turns love relationships into manipulation. From birth, children need love and support. Most of these problems come from present-life issues; only a few come from past lives. Some children have a panic within themselves because of past life issues of abandonment.

Typically, a child is born with the attitude, "Here I am. Love me." It is important for a child to bond with parents as well as siblings. When something happens to break a child's trust, such as an abusive or absent parent, that child will have a difficult time bonding with others.

As children grow and mature, they begin to explore ties with other people. Some of these experiences go smoothly, and some do not. Whatever goes well is marvelous and good. It builds self-esteem, so children learn how to create relationships. Then children can wisely decide, through a process of evaluation, whether or not to continue a relationship. "I know you are someone I can connect with but you are not whom my heart desires." They learn to distinguish between physical and emotional connections.

Even when connections are both physical and emotional, the mind may realize that is not possible. It is

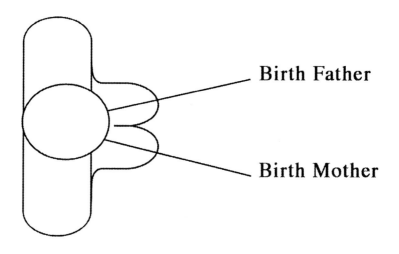

Figure 11 – "V" Connecting Parents to Children

important for children to become discerning, so they can decide their future wisely.

A child has strong and independent chakras that connect in a "V" to both parents **Figure 11**. When one parent is not in a child's life, one arm of the "V" never attaches. This is why people who grew up with only one parent sometimes cannot totally partner with the opposite sex. This dysfunction merely means that they cannot bond in a relationship as closely as other couples. It does not necessarily mean they will become a homosexual, although this could be the choice for this lifetime.

If parentless children had two loving parents during their childhood, they would better understand how relationships work. But, if children cannot develop one of their connections, the result is a dangling or wavering arm of the "V." As adults they must make a conscious decision to work on their issues. If they do not, they truly will not know how to be in a productive love union.

Love is the most important energy for children. Loving parents can be fairly ineffective and still raise loving children. This is not the best situation, but it can work if the children understand they are loved. Children and parents have chosen this lesson, so their souls can progress in this lifetime.

It is important for parents and children to remain close. Initially, the mother is closest to her child. The mother was a child's primary connection in previous generations. Since fathers are bonding much better these days, the "Vs" are better balanced. Instead of having one wide arm "V" for the mother and a narrow arm for the father, the child will have two, strong, and wide bonds to both parents. A strong bond with both parents does not mean a child will be under their thumbs, although it could be the soul's choice for this lifetime. Strong "V" connections help the children learn relationships and understand feelings. When the time comes, children can appropriately separate from their parents and move on. Becoming an individual is necessary in a healthy parent-child relationship.

While it is important for children to loosen their chakra connection with parents so they may become more independent, it is also important for them to maintain links. Instead of children's connections to parents remaining like thick branches, they become like thin cords, ropes, or threads. The strength of the tie depends on how close the children are to their parents.

The job of parents is to raise children to disconnect from their parents and live independent lives. For children to be successful, they need to separate emotionally from their parents. The situation of children who stay bonded for years without disengaging is very sad.

Parents and children have a distinct link that will continue all their lives through the heart chakra. If the family remains strong, they will have both strong heart and moderately strong intuitive chakra connections.

When the relationship between parents and children is weak or indifferent, the children's heart chakras do not connect, just the intuitive chakra. The remaining chakras are only partially connected. To reunite the heart chakra with the family requires work that, unfortunately, many parents and children are not willing to do.

When children are grown, they should remain somewhat connected, yet separate from a negative parent for their own soul's progress. To separate physically is one way to handle the situation, but the relationship would be better if the children only emotionally separate, so their parents do not control them. The chakras must stay connected, because they are the links of love. Even though parents can create chaos in the lives of their children, children can love their parents.

Only when parents cause continuous physical or emotional harm should children free themselves 100 percent from their parents. Even then, it is important to maintain a tie with their parents, if only through the occasional exchange of a greeting card. This limited contact can continue until parents and children truly understand their relationship.

Adopted children connect to both their birth and adopted parents with double "V" attachments coming from the chakras **Figure 12**. One set of "Vs" is for the adoptive parents and the other is for the birth parents.

The physical and emotional connections of birth mothers for their children are fairly strong. Sometimes

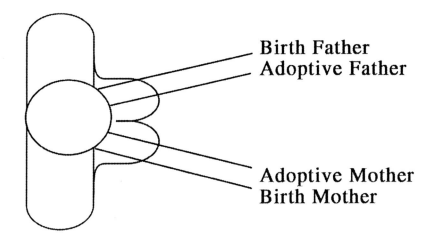

Figure 12 – "V" Connecting Birth and Adoptive Parents to Children

birth fathers are distant or not involved; therefore, the connective "Vs" of these fathers are weaker.

Infants and small children bond easily with their adoptive parents. Older children must understand that their birth parents are not available or are considered unable to parent; otherwise, they will not connect with the adoptive parents as easily.

If the adoptive parents are caring people, they develop strong "Vs" with their adopted children. However, the "Vs" from the birth parents are left hanging on these children. **Adopted children know they are adopted**

because they have a yearning in their auras and in their chakras to complete the "Vs" connection to their biological family.

Simply meeting with their birth parents completes these "Vs" connections to their chakras. When the birth parents are deceased, the "V" may extend like branches of a tree to the birth parents' extended families, so these children can experience some of the love the biological parents would have given. Even though the bond is not as direct and as strong as a "V" to the birth parents, the connection is a bond. It is important for adopted children to complete this link with their biological family.

When children are small, they are drawn into their parents' egg-shaped aura. Until it is time for them to separate, this egg-like tie continues. Then the chakras stay only minimally connected. When parents and children come together again, the egg reconnects. This is why children say, "When I am around my parents, I act like a child."

When parents age, the egg connection flip-flops. Parents become more childlike, and children become the adults. **When the auric egg reverses, many parents become dependent upon their children.** Then children have the larger aura and their parents the smaller one.

Elderly

All people have both positive and negative traits within them. Yet, most people try to be loving, which is extremely important. Many old people become nasty, protective, and fearful, because their chakras are dangling and their auras are weak and wavy. This causes them to become aggressive. These behavior changes do not make them bad; they just make them who they are. Dealing with frail elderly parents can be difficult. If these parents were belligerent young people, their children should not be surprised at their older parents' negative behavior.

In Alzheimer's disease this behavior becomes more pronounced. Your friend's mother, Phyllis, who had Alzheimer's disease, behaved in a way she would not have done normally. Prior to developing Alzheimer's, she did not behave negatively, but she would think negative thoughts. This is why her negative behavior manifested later.

When someone advances through Alzheimer's, their auric, chemical, and chakra connections begin to erratically disintegrate. There is a degree of connection but it is not what it once was. The chakra connections are the size of sewing threads. Eventually, when the chakras completely disconnect, the person dies.

Travel and the Body

Traveling creates challenges for your body's auric energy. The Earth rotates on its axis at one speed. When you are walking, you are able to adjust with each step. The length of your walk may affect your endurance, but the Earth's spin has no real effect.

On the other hand, riding in a vehicle or a train moves your body faster. While the spin of the Earth has some effect, the bouncing and vibrating of your auric energy, as you ride, causes you fatigue. *For example, when someone is ready to return home from the hospital, she may feel much better than the day of her operation. However, even though the ride home is a short distance, it will wear her out, so she needs to rest.*

Flying in an airplane puts additional stresses on the body. The direction of the plane and its vibrations affect our auric energy. A plane going in the direction of the Earth's spin causes one to feel fatigue, while a plane going in the opposite direction of the Earth's spin causes a person even more fatigue. Flying creates double problems for our auric energy.

When you travel, your body's aura becomes "out of sync." Upon arriving at your destination, you need time to readjust your auric energy.

Chapter Six

Blue Level Energy

Speaking, knowing, self-confidence, self-knowing, self-love

Your Soul

This is important for everyone to know. Love exists on many levels. God's love for you is infinite and wondrous. God cannot become angry with you because God loves your soul. God knows your soul, not as you think you are, but as the beautiful soul you truly are. The soul resides in the physical and auric bodies. Your soul also resides during all your lifetimes and into infinity.

When you make mistakes or commit so-called sins in your life, as you call them, these are your lessons to learn. God sees these mistakes, but does not judge them. God knows your soul is wondrous. When you die, you are the one who judges your actions, thoughts, and words. You have a freewill choice to do what you wish in this lifetime. However, this choice may be affected by previous lifetimes. Your current lifetime will also affect how you proceed in future lifetimes—what you will do and what you will need to learn.

Others describe the soul as being outside the body. Your definition of soul, Linda, is within the body. In reality, you are all right. Yes, the body is inhabited by the soul during this lifetime. But, the soul is bigger, because the soul is more than just in the body.

Some people describe the soul as beyond the exterior parameters of the physical body. The soul is bigger than the person, because the soul extends beyond the body and evolves for eternity.

A person's projected aura is a combination of the soul and body energies, which can extend up to several feet around the person. The surrounding aura is a radiation of the extended energy. The human personality is where the soul resides during this lifetime.

Some say all souls were perfect from the beginning. If we were perfect, why do we have to incarnate?

In the beginning of creation, all souls were created equally and simultaneously. They did not have emotions, knowledge, lessons, or any of the other aspects required for soul growth. Your souls were as perfect as empty shells.

With each lifetime experience on Earth, on other planets, or other realms in the universe, the soul continues to develop. The soul's shell is filled with the achievement of unconditional love from each consecutive lifetime or each existence. The records of all your lifetimes are included in the Akashic Record. When you strive toward unconditional love, you fill the internal level of your soul's shell. Loving is part of who you are and what you can be. The expansiveness of your love fills the shell.

So, before that?

You had no experience.

In this realm or other realms?

In any realm.

What your soul strives to do is to fill the shell with your unconditional love, not with the heaviness of emotion that is part of the Earth experience. For example, let's use a pitcher for each individual soul's lifetime. The individual manifests on Earth as an empty pitcher with possibly some residue of other lifetimes in the bottom. Since the Earth experience includes various emotional and physical events, it is extremely challenging for that soul.

When you die, the pitcher is left in various degrees or stages of color. The vast majority of people evolve from mud to clearer water or they go from sludge to something clearer. When people totally rid themselves of anger, controlling emotions, and lack of forgiveness and become unconditionally loving, the pitcher will hold pure, clear water. Even though the goal of humans in each lifetime is to create clear, pure water, few people succeed.

Some souls will have come far, even if they died with anger the color of deep red cherry juice in their pitcher. Some may have progressed to the point of a loving aspect— clear, pink rose water. To lighten the soul's color, this person has faced many challenges and addressed them. She also might have learned forgiveness or other lessons, which are important for the soul's growth.

Do you see how well the soul process works? Individuals need to understand that as life progresses, they must move forward for their soul's growth. **The goal of each individual's lifetime is to become as unconditionally loving as they are able by forgiving, eliminating anger, and accepting both themselves and others unconditionally**. When this is done, the soul is finished with the humanness. It moves on to other levels of work on the other side. Although reaching this point is difficult, it can be achieved.

Your body is the manifestation of soul. Over time, the soul has evolved as plants, rocks, and animals prior to developing into a wondrous human. This is also why you have a love for certain plants or animals. The first time a soul manifests as a human, it has a great deal to learn. The soul has less to learn because of its prior existence as an animal. As a herd animal, you learned a basic need to connect to the pack. As a cat, you learn independence, a necessary lesson for becoming human.

Linda, you love lions, elephants, flowers, and the magnificence of the trees because you were all these things formerly. These prior connections are the reason you are attracted to those animals and plants.

In past lives, you were only a few water animals, even though your mother says you swim like a polar bear. If you had been a polar bear, you would take to water more easily. You find swimming in the cleanliness of pools more enjoyable than lakes with their vegetation.

Your lives as water animals were short, and you drowned as a person in another life. Even though you enjoy being around water, you are not totally comfortable in it. But you are comfortable with emotions, the symbolism of water. You have a great love of dogs but not horses. You were never a horse, but you were a deer, a gazelle, and a lion.

Various lifetime preferences come from an affinity with animals, plants, rocks, trees, and locations based on what we were prior to becoming human. Souls progress through these various stages in order to prepare for humanness.

When you feel good about yourself, your chakras extend out into the universe to the radius of your aura, which can be anywhere from 1 to 2 feet or many feet out into the room.

. On days when you are feeling less confident, your chakras and aura draw closer to the body. When you feel depressed, all your chakras close down or recede into the body, especially your crown and your intuitive chakras.

Love of self is very important. The throat or fifth chakra is most important in self-love. The heart chakra is second and the intuitive is third, followed by the remaining chakras. When you have a high degree of self-love, the energy of your fifth chakra glows. When your self-love is low, your throat chakra displays only a low light.

Self-love is important, so you can joyfully live life. If you do not love yourself, decisions are based on fear. When you are fearful of being who you are, you cannot be yourself.

There are times, Linda, when you need to be yourself and say what you really feel. Other times, you need to hold back, and you do. Sometimes you hold back too much. You should absolutely say more when you need to speak up.

When things go wrong in your life, you are being challenged to grow. Challenges create an option of growth and change. If everything were always wonderful, great, and fantastic, your soul would not progress. If you die without having learned from your challenges, your soul would advance little from being alive.

Fortunately, many people change for the better in subtle ways. Humans are not perfect; if they were, they would not have manifested. Humans must strive to unconditionally love. The Earth teaches lessons in a definitive way. If we stand up for ourselves, positively believe in ourselves, and think of ourselves as loving and wonderful "gifts of the Universe," then we will handle all that comes our way.

When you love yourself, you make wise decisions based on what is good for you — not choices based on pride, arrogance, aggressiveness, or non-assertiveness. You make wise decisions that advance your soul.

There are many degrees of pride. Pride has been considered one of the seven deadly sins, because it causes blind behavior. Pride can hurt you and others in many ways. However, pride can come from doing something well: "I am proud of what I have achieved." And, you can have pride in your children's accomplishments whatever they may be. If kept in proportion, these are positive types of pride.

Self-love is magnificent, wondrous, and necessary for soul growth. Then, all your experiences and decisions are determined by how you perceive and love yourself. Loving yourself is wonderful and positive.

The Earth will become totally loving when everyone makes decisions based on love rather than selfishness, which is something all humans deal with daily. Every selfless act, such as donating time to some cause or assisting a person to succeed, is extremely important for your soul's growth.

God cares deeply for you and all you do, for you are indeed magnificent children of the universe. You are love. You are loving. You are lovable and you are loved. This is the essence of all human beings. This is the essence of why you are sent to the Earth — to love unconditionally.

The Aura

The aura works in conjunction with chemical and chakra connections. Chakra energy comes from separate energy centers in the body; the aura is the energy of the whole body. Loving auras project in a positive way.

Almost everyone in your life is from a previous lifetime. If you have positive chakra, chemical, and auric connections with people, your auras blend. Most often, they blend when the auras make contact with another person. This is why it is so difficult to separate from a person with whom you have had a previous chemistry connection. The relationship may be over, but the attraction is still there.

When you understand negative relationships, you are better able to accomplish separation in this lifetime; otherwise, you will have to deal with this attraction again in another lifetime.

Blue Level Energy

There are mixed feelings about soul-mate relationships. Many feel that finding your soul mate gives you wonderful compatibility, and, therefore, a wonderful life. Others believe that relationships need challenges in order to grow and learn. Challenges brought to a soul-mate couple are worked through together. Soul mates meet challenges with a more united agenda.

When there is no soul-mate chemistry, two people have to deal with both their own issues and the challenge of being a couple. Since you grow from both situations, one is no better or no worse than the other.

Your aura expands and contracts according to your energy level. When you are charismatic, your energy extends like a balloon into your aura.

When our energy initially joined with you, Linda, you had enlarged your aura to accept our energy. The dog sitting beside you could feel our energy, so it moved because we were in your aura. We connected with you, but not directly into your body, like a funnel. When you meditate, we connect into your drifting auric body through your spiritual and intuitive chakras.

At the time you were walking through the Las Vegas casino looking for your husband, you noticed that people seated at tables several feet ahead turned around to look at you. Your directness projected your auric energy forward. Your physical body energy and your auric energy extended like a laser beam; therefore, it affected people seated at the tables.

Charisma is the extension of the body's energy toward people. When you give speeches, Linda, your charisma projects many feet into the room. Whether you are speaking or singing, your crown and throat chakras project. When you link with your intuitive and spiritual chakras, you are connecting with the universe.

Linda, you do not have the maximum amount of charisma, because it would overpower you. But you have magnificent chemical and auric connections to people, and charisma that attracts others. You have enough charisma so people will listen to and hear you, but not so much that they are drawn in blindly.

Charisma is also a source of power that can be used positively or negatively. When the loss of power becomes fear and turns negative, it takes over a person's whole body. If someone chooses to use their charismatic power in a negative way, he draws people into a web, like the cult leader Jim Jones, who attracted people to his beliefs by teaching social justice and racial equality mixed with Biblical scripture. When he was overcome by his power and

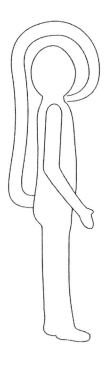

Figure 13 – Charisma Becoming Negative Power

began to fear its loss, his chakras turned negative by quietly coming up and over his head and into his back at the root **Figure 13**. In the end, Jones moved nearly 700 people to Guyana, where he then convinced them to commit mass suicide.

The Love of Children

The love of parent and child is different from the love expressed by a couple. The love between a parent and child is a close physical bond. To have the close love of a child is the goal for all parents. At conception, the father's energy connects with the mother to make the child. There is a more direct energy bond with the body of the mother because of the pregnancy. When a child is born, she is most often loved because of this energy bond with the parents.

Since connections with children begin with conception, parental rejection wounds the child deeply and creates a broken energy bond. It is important for parents to love and connect with the children, so they can grow. When infants are handled during their diaper changes, they connect with their base chakras in a physical way. It feels good for babies to rid themselves of the weight and smell of their diapers.

It is important that the many bonds, which initially link children to their parents, eventually are broken. Of all the chakras, the most important one to separate in a parent-child relationship is the partnership or second chakra. Once accomplished, children can grow and live their own lives.

When children have healthy self-esteem and are totally independent, their chakras are very strong. **In fact, all the chakra areas are enhanced in individuals with good self-esteem.**

Blue Level Energy

As children grow, first they must disengage the spiritual or the crown chakra areas from both parents. Because children are a part of their parents and understand how to manipulate them, the bond is incredibly strong. Most children instinctively know that they must disconnect. Even though separating from parents is important, independence is still difficult for children to accomplish. This process begins around three-and-a-half years and continues onward. Children both connect to and disconnect from their parents continually.

Children need to disengage a portion of their heart ties that link them to their parents, so they are independent enough to go to school. Their self-confidence chakra needs to disconnect from parental concerns or fears, so children can go out and face the world. The base chakra, or survival area, needs to detach in teenagers, so they can survive without their parents and pursue their life's work.

Children's base chakra actually separates and reconnects over and over again because of their need for personal survival. Even though these ties ultimately detach, children still feel an affinity for their parents. Their connection to parents has erotic overtones around puberty, but this quickly disappears, so they can move on. When children disengage from their parents, they continue to grow as people.

Independence is necessary for children. **Loving your children does not always mean loving their behavior.** Sometimes teenagers become rebellious. Typical teenage rebellion is an attempt to establish their own identity and to separate from their parents. Teenagers with either overbearing or uninvolved parents often act out to a greater degree. It is important for you as a parent to let go of your parental connection, so your child can grow into an independent person.

For example, one of your sons, Linda, used a sharp knife, and the other used a dull ax, to separate from you. When a child uses a dull ax, he feels a strong firm connection to his parents. *Let me explain: our second son was born with medical problems, so we became very close. He worked longer at separating than did his brother.*

A parent can create a strong bond, but these ties can cause additional challenges. When a parent's hold is overly strong, it is difficult for a child to break away. Sometimes it takes years to separate completely from a parent. Often, it is difficult for parents to loosen their connections because of the large amount of time, energy, and concern they have invested in their children. It is best for both to allow the process to proceed to completion.

Love and Past Lives

Parents and children are connected from past lives. They bring each other challenges for this lifetime. Some parents create difficulties for their children; some are extremely negative. It is important for children to grow past parental challenges. Even loving parents can limit the growth of their children, which creates problems for each child in the family.

Every person in your life is important. As we said, some people you meet will be new to your soul in this lifetime. Generally, during your current lifetime, you will not work with all the souls from your former lifetimes.

You carry over some issues from one lifetime to another, but it is the challenges of this lifetime that you are here to learn. Most of your past lessons move forward as positive memories. A few memories consist of fears from previous lifetimes, such as your personal issue, Linda, of swimming in water with vegetation, as we discussed previously. Generally, your memories are positive. These include wonderful places where you have lived, joyous activities, people, and events from various lifetimes. They are only a fraction of your total memories.

Your personality in this lifetime learns constantly from the people in your life. Generally, as a human your soul does a wonderful job of learning and moving the soul forward. **Unconditional love is the soul's reason for becoming human again.**

Friendship love comes from a connection with other people from past lives. Friends are your support system. They give moral support, so you can do what you need to do and be the person you need to be.

For instance, you and your friend Sharon were sisters in a past life. You understand who she is and why she does what she does. Currently, she is enveloped in her job, but this will soon calm down. In the near future, she will relocate her entire operation to the home office. The move will be good for her because she needs to be closer to home, a place she finds calming. Commuting is hard on her body.

You and your friend Isabelle were not sisters in a past life; you were friends. This friendship is delicate, because she is in a fragile space in this life. You were closer friends in another lifetime. It is good you are friends with her in this life, because she needs spiritual friends. She also needs time by herself to recharge after being around people. Her major illness has created many issues for her and her husband.

Your acquaintance Myra is a pleasant person. You were not friends in a past life, just acquaintances. While this relationship has been maintained in this life, the friendship she would like must be on her terms, not on mutually agreeable terms. This is unfortunate, because you could be good friends. She does not understand your non-traditional, expanded religious beliefs, and she rejects people who do not believe as she does. Acceptance of others' beliefs is part of her lesson for this life.

Barbara was a nursemaid to you in another life; therefore, she cares for you. She is a sensitive person and cares how people react. She is living with a difficult husband who does not raise her self-esteem, but she has learned to handle it in the best way possible. Her club membership is important to her, because there she can be the focal point instead of her husband, who demands constant attention.

Your husband was your student in a former life and is still learning from you. Your job is to gently teach him. His job is to give you space to grow spiritually. Your children also learn from you and were involved in your past lives.

Chapter Seven

Indigo Level Energy

Intuition, networking, unity, mass consciousness, universe

Unconditional Love

Without love, people do not flourish; they stagnate and withdraw into themselves. Therefore, it is important that connections are physical as well as emotional. Meaningful connections are necessary for personal growth. They are not just a part of living. People must learn to love themselves and others. Even though 100 percent unconditional love 100 percent of the time is not probable because you are human, you can accept other people and not reject them based on face value—on their appearance, looks, their skin color, or what they project. You may feel reticent about others, but you should not reject them as human beings.

For example, I know a man, Martin, who makes judgments about people based on their looks. While he was staying at a motel, he decided the housekeepers were lesbians. When he returned to his room after getting an ice cream cone, his door was ajar. He was sure the housekeeping staff was trying to steal something because to him, "That's what those people (homosexuals/lesbians) do."

This way of thinking is difficult for you to understand, Linda, because you are not a person who automatically rejects. You are a person who looks, evaluates, and says: "I can get along; I can't get along; I am comfortable; I am uncomfortable; I can work with this person, or I cannot work with this person." You evaluate and strive to treat a person with respect.

People must realize that automatic rejection of another person hurts their own souls, not the other person. People are the way they are because of their life experiences. Just accept them.

When my friend Rita was a newlywed, she was introduced to all the people in her husband's small hometown. When asked what she thought of everyone, she indicated that she enjoyed meeting them all. However, she found "Joe" to be a bit different. Her mother-in-law explained Joe's history. When Rita heard of his life's challenges, she understood why Joe behaved the way he did.

People who reject others in a negative and/or violent way create adverse situations for themselves, either in this lifetime or a future one. People should understand that relationships create wonderful bonds that assist people in their soul's progress. People, who isolate themselves from others by not interrelating, harm themselves. Most people are not meant to come to Earth and live alone in a hut in the middle of nowhere. They could do that anywhere in the universe.

Earth is where people must learn to get along with others through harmony and joy. **It is important for you to realize that no one in this world is better or worse than anyone else.** Try to get along with people in a positive way. This means letting people express themselves, respecting them, and saying in a positive manner whether you agree or disagree with their opinion.

Sometimes people allow themselves to become involved in negative situations, which others use against them. Some people, however, are put in compromising positions because a malicious person does not like them. At times, the person whose job is compromised is not even the real target. Nonetheless, having a job politically destroyed, although hurtful, is an opportunity for soul growth.

Unfortunately, the political process in the American government during the late 1990s was very divisive. People chose to be mean-spirited and to hurt one another. Part of the U. S. government's political turmoil came from the other lifetimes of all participants, but most of it came from this lifetime. In this age of in-depth investigation, information is often revealed in a negative manner. When an investigation turns malicious, it creates negative karma for the investigators and for the person investigated, in either this or a future lifetime. Investigators must choose to reveal their information honestly and positively.

The most important human process is learning to love unconditionally. Some people believe the highest type of love is either romantic or sexual. Unconditional love, however, is the highest and most difficult type of love to achieve. Sometimes we succeed in achieving it with many people, but not with everyone.

Unconditional love is not achieved by smiling at everyone, throwing your arms around them, and giving them hugs and kisses. It does not even mean that you converse. Ideally, it means you are totally accepting and understanding of everyone; in reality, unconditional love is accepting others as they are.

No one accepts others unconditionally 100 percent of the time because of the prejudices that exist from an individual's background. Whether you recognize them or not, prejudices are a part of who you are.

Every person is equally important. You must be open and accept each person. This means that your heart remains open, so you can accept others without fear. However, your intuition must remain aware, so you are sensitive to dangerous situations. Your spiritual and intuitive chakras should stay open, so you can evaluate whether other connections can be made.

When you converse, the chakras of emotion and conversation are involved. When you pass by people, you sense their presence through your intuitive and crown chakras. A person's aura can be felt by just being around them. Physically, unconditional love creates a connection between people's energy centers.

Friendly people extend their chakras and auras continually. Unconditional love is like saying, "I do not know who you are, but I am willing to be open and accept you, whether you are homeless, rich, poor, or mean. I will try to accept who you are." This is a challenge. Unconditional love is very simple but often difficult to achieve.

Those who cannot love in this way have to ask themselves: "What is *my* problem? Do I feel physically threatened? Am I afraid because I do not understand what is going on? Do I have fear because this person is different? What is it that I am not willing to accept? Are they richer or poorer than I? Why can't I accept them?" Once you understand the reasons for your reactions, you are on your way to unconditional love.

Sensitive people feel a lack of energy from closed people who cannot love unconditionally. Even though you may not connect to everyone, you can accept whatever energy people project.

Addictions

When the heart and intuitive chakras are emotionally hurt, addictions are created. Whether the addiction is gambling, food, liquor, money, sex, drugs, objects, etc., addictions are linked strongly to the emotional (fourth) and intuitive (sixth) chakras, but most strongly to the self-confidence (fifth) chakra.

When the intuitive and self-confidence chakras intertwine and grow into one another, they feel like tentacles attaching to the self. Although these tentacles are extremely difficult to remove, it can be done carefully, with love and kindness. When you are angry with yourself, you decrease your self-confidence. Learning to love yourself breaks the addiction; emotional anger is changed by love.

Addictions emanate different auric colors. The addictive heart emotion emanates an intense black-green. When love lightens the black-green until it becomes a true green, highlighted by the white light of God's love, the addict can break free from his addiction.

The love of food is intuitive for you, Linda. Your food addiction comes, partly, from the habit of nibbling on something after school. You are beginning to let go of the fear from your second chakra with partnership and working relationships. *Besides having my job politically destroyed, I had a club of "friends," led by another, turn on me because I questioned one member's desire to change the direction of the group.* When you can look at yourself with love and fully recognize God's love for you, your fear will be eliminated.

For many people, addictions stem from the self-confidence chakra. People's physical addiction to alcohol is the result of a karmic chemical imbalance in the body. Even though this addictive imbalance is acceptable in your culture, people must learn to eliminate their dependency on liquor. The imbalance can be changed through love, diet, and the elimination of fear. People must always be aware of the chemical imbalance that makes them prone to addiction. When they commit to eliminating this problem, they can handle their alcohol addiction.

Commercial tobacco is strongly addictive. A relaxing break in the day and oral comfort are also a part of tobacco addiction. Chemical companies have aided tobacco companies by developing ingredients to make tobacco even more addictive. Eventually, the tobacco and additives cause illness.

Your friend Marsha once said, "Native Americans who smoke peace pipes don't become addicted" because they smoke only natural, not the chemically tainted tobacco.

All habits are hard to break. Experts say habits can be made or broken in three weeks. Giving up a habit is difficult because it fulfills a personal need.

Drug addictions that cause people to have hallucinations or "highs" are attempts to escape from pain by moving into an altered state. Drug addictions influence the crown and intuitive chakras. Some users believe drugs connect their spiritual centers. When drugs are used too often, people destroy numerous brain cells. **People must learn to build their self-confidence, so they can handle life's challenges and conquer their addictions.**

The Equality of Nations

Some people say, "We are the best because our nation is superior." In essence, all mankind should try to love and understand one another. Just as no person is better than another, no nation is any better than another nation. Each country can choose to develop because each is equal in potential ability and in the sight of God.

A dictator needs his people to remain controlled, downtrodden, and poor, so he can maintain power. Dictators provide little opportunity for people to grow as individuals. More positive forms of government encourage people to evolve, so they can improve their status and skills.

For some nations, improving their status means improving their cleanliness, health, and trade. If this is accomplished, the nation, tribe, and family will benefit. Nations need to interact with other countries. Nations that try to isolate themselves prohibit their people from having new experiences. Nations must evaluate other options and decide if they should incorporate new ideas. **Democratic nations strive to improve themselves, often through education.**

Sometimes people who live in ghettos or low-income neighborhoods suffer from oppression and anger. When they feel alienated, they are unable to improve themselves. Therefore, they believe society is prohibiting their chances for improvement. This is unfortunate, because everyone can choose to improve. Someone once said, "I have never seen a homeowner who is a drive-by shooter." This is essentially true. If people feel impoverished and unfulfilled, their anger prohibits them from bettering themselves. Often they will not try to improve.

A few people understand that the way out of these neighborhoods is through education. Unfortunately, some of these people are killed before they can leave. Although the victims' deaths are sad for the families, their souls were here for a universal lesson—to show that there are positive people in every aspect of society.

Often, parents teach children to be careful around people from cultures different from their own, because the parents are uncomfortable around them. They teach children to be fearful in unfamiliar situations. When children are taught fear, they grow fearful of others. But if children understand that positive and negative people exist in all societies, then children will learn caution and use their evaluative skills.

Caution and fear are two different attitudes. Caution means that no matter where children are in this world, they need to be aware of their surroundings. Whether in another country, an American city, or in their own neighborhood, they should always be cautious, because there are positive and negative people living everywhere. Being cautious is different from saying you must watch out for "them" because they are a different race, religion, or nationality.

It is important for all to realize that everyone on Earth has a potential for good or evil. The potential for evil is not innate. Evil is taught.

Negative people are not innately bad. They are negative, because, over the years, they have been deeply hurt or adversely affected by the decisions and actions of their parents or other people in their lives. Instead of rising above their problems, they become traumatized. As we said, it is important for people to understand their unique personalities, so they can make conscious decisions for their soul's growth.

Love and the Universe

Love is a universal force, not just an earthly one. There are life forms in the universe which do not experience love because love is feeling, and they are emotionless.

Some people say being emotionless is more highly evolved; others say it is less highly evolved. Being emotionless is neither; it is how they are. How they relate is different from the emotional love that exists on Earth.

The human understanding of the universe is that love is forever and eternal. Actually, love is everywhere in the universe, but not every being in the universe is as loving as those on Earth. Generally, these beings get along, but some are more positive than others. There are aliens who are occasionally negative, but they are very rare.

Love is expressed differently here on Earth than it would be expressed on Mars, Jupiter, or in other solar systems. There, love is not as emotional; it is not a basic part of their nature. They experience love on a different level.

Generally, aliens are loving entities who work with other parts of the universe to distribute information. This is difficult for some humans to understand. Some travel in spaceships and some do not. They visit places in the universe through their thought processes. When aliens stay on Earth, they are able to manifest as humans. They often come to help people in various situations and to dispense loving information; then they disappear.

Aliens act and react the same way people do, but they are not people. Aliens are entities from other solar systems. They assume the characteristics of whatever community they are visiting; Earth is one such community. Aliens usually come for a couple of years or a minimum of six months. There is no way to tell them by the shape of their face, their head, or by any other feature, because they blend in. They often do not require the sleep humans do. Some aliens come for scientific or exploratory purposes.

The majority of aliens are here to monitor humans and to spread love. They show tremendous love to people. They work in a nonaggressive way. They give moral support to the people they help. Aliens will take a job and work in an area. The only way you will know they are aliens is that they are transient. They come to do their good work of building love and move on. This is part of their karmic work.

Aliens come to areas of major crisis to smooth over the tensions of communities and countries. They do not work in an overt way, but work in a gentle and kind way. This is only a fraction of the love being spread throughout the universe. There are many areas on Earth that are unloving and in need of love.

In the Mideast, aliens are trying to assist the peace process between the Palestinians and the Israelis. The negativity that has built up over the whole situation is intense, which makes it difficult for them to work.

Why aren't more aliens sent to bring balance to the area?

Aliens are not sent to change the area. Their work is to guide a region to become more loving. Negative forces can easily undo the good that has progressed.

Why are negative forces allowed to prevail?

Negativity is strongly directed energy. Love is a gentler, kinder energy, but love is the stronger force, which will overcome in the end. For example, if someone rushed up to you and declared his love on first meeting, you might be overwhelmed. But getting to know him gently can convince you of his love. This is also how aliens work, kindly and gently.

Aliens and angels are different. All angels are aspects of God. **Angels are here to give specific messages and moral support to people.** They manifest as an energy, a light, an odor, a voice, or as a real presence, but they are fleeting. During a crisis, they stay in our presence only for as long as they are needed.

Chapter Eight

Violet Level Energy

Transformation

God and the Chakras

Divine energy connects to all your chakras. Your love and openness with God establish a major spiritual connection through the crown chakra. The other chakras open like the "V" of a fan. The crown and the third-eye chakras are directly connected to God.

When people die, the chakras start to diminish. Instead of being the diameter of a tree trunk, they diminish to the diameter of a little branch. As they shrink or diminish in length, they are unable to connect with people. The chakras diminish until they withdraw into the body. At this point, the soul will finally leave the body, and death occurs.

The soul is not electrical energy; it is spiritual energy. Electrical energy, although greatly diminished, can remain within the body longer. Spiritual energy withdraws from the chakras and limbs of the body when you die. The configuration of the soul is similar to a little mist cloud. The soul is not a cloud, but this is how it is visualized.

The weight of the soul is minuscule, a fraction of an ounce. **The soul is your real being, your real essence, or true self.**

Predictions

God has an innate, wondrous, definitive, and marvelous love for you. God sees the love you have for other people and how you treat them, whether they are your spouse, children, friends, or the rest of mankind. The acceptance and the unconditional love you project are most important. When people evolve and become 100 percent unconditionally loving, then and only then will mankind, as you know it, cease to exist.

There have been projections and predictions about when this will occur. In fact, how people act and react to one another changes the timing on those predictions and projections. When mankind is loving, the timeline moves forward. The doomsday predictors are saying that life will fall apart in the near future. Life will not fall apart. Life will continue on a different level — a very different level.

For instance, the good that Oprah Winfrey is doing by teaching people about unconditional love is very important. We must understand that love is universal and is not exclusive to human beings. Since the Earth is based on emotion, love is expressed in different ways. Love can be acceptance, romantic love, or merely affection.

It is important that you understand how love affects and wonderfully changes people. Eventually, when all humans become loving, the Earth's energy will change. Yes, catastrophic events will continue to happen, so people can experience the joy of giving and of loving, as well as the challenges.

You read a book that mentioned the theory of survival of the fittest. It questioned whether it is right to give food and aid to starving people in an area. Our answer is twofold. It is important to know that some people will not survive, so the situation can be brought to the world's attention. All the Earth's resources cannot be concentrated into one area. But, when help is sent, it is wonderful. So you must understand: Those who have previously died, have died for a cause; those who have survived, have survived out of love. Although this is a difficult concept for many people to accept, you must understand that everything happens in its rightful order.

This was the case for the starving people in Ethiopia several years ago. Because of the masses of people involved, love could not be expressed to everyone, so many did not survive. The people who survived were the ones who were supposed to survive. The love expressed by those who gave was magnificent. Whether participants, aid workers, or donors, all souls chose their part in the process before manifesting.

Summary

Mankind has a variety of connections that are real — chakra, auric, rubber bands, chemical. The feelings that humans have are created and broken by the connections you feel and do not feel. When you understand the positive and negative use of power, then you can understand the importance of the equal connections between people. When power is equal and shared, two people can grow as a couple or as individuals.

All of mankind is striving to understand the basic question, "Why? Why is mankind acting and behaving this way? Why am I acting this way? Why do I feel this way? Why do I think as I think? Why do I say what I say? Why am I here?" Hearing facts is different from understanding them. Understanding gives an individual depth. It is most important to understand "Why?"

When you learn that you are here to understand your emotions and to learn to love yourself and others unconditionally, then you have given yourself a marvelous gift. This gift will help your soul to lovingly progress. Strive to live as lovingly as possible, knowing that you will be challenged from time to time.

The soul is on an important path of growth. If the person decides to deal with the challenges it's been given, then the soul moves forward with joy and love. All people are working toward the same goal—to learn to love unconditionally. Humans have a difficult time loving everyone unconditionally because of the prejudices that exist among all peoples and tribes.

Unconditional love occurs when you understand how your emotions affect you. They are the essence of your humanness. The vast majority of issues you will face are from your present life. Only 5 or 10 percent of your issues come from previous lifetimes. Very few children are born with major issues carried over from previous lifetimes.

It is important for all people to understand that loving one another is God's suggestion, God's direction, and God's desire for mankind. When mankind loves unconditionally, humans will no longer have to manifest on Earth. Instead, your souls will continue to manifest in other realms for other learning experiences.

God loves and cares for everyone. Everyone is encompassed within God's purview, His total acceptance. Since God sees your struggles as moving your soul toward unconditional love, there is no judging. God does not judge your soul; each soul moves toward its potential of unconditional love at different rates of speed.

Summary

Since the millennium changeover, more people are moving more directly toward a loving existence. As they move in this direction, they become magnificent.

God holds a special joy in His heart for humans. God loves. God is loving. God is lovable. God is love. Amen.

Epilogue

*Now you are a part of my journey
of* **The Letter of Love.**

*Take what you want from the book and
freely share its concept
of unconditional love with others.*

*Please visit my web site at
www.letteroflove.com
to share your personal growth from reading*
The Letter of Love.

*Together, we can change the future
by becoming catalysts for unconditional love.*

Peace, joy, and love,

Linda

Exploratory Questions

These questions are for your exploration or as points of discussion with a friend, group of friends, or a formal discussion group. There are no correct answers. Let the questions reveal to you what you believe and why you react as you do. Use this information to evaluate how unconditionally loving you are or would like to be.

Chapter One — The Chakras and Relationships

Have you ever been blinded by romantic love? What happened to open your eyes? How has this knowledge affected your relationships?

Have you ever experienced chemistry? If so, how did it feel different from romantic love? Was the chemistry positive or negative? If negative, how did it end? What are your feelings now?

Have you ever been in a relationship where one partner discouraged the growth of another? How did you react? What did you do to overcome the discouragement?

Describe the difference between a romantic and a platonic relationship you have experienced with someone of the opposite sex.

Chapter Two — Red Level Energy

Physical sex, release, forgiveness, power, physical astuteness, action

Think back to when you found something you collect. What did you feel physically?

Do you like your job? As much as you used to? Do you need a change? If so, what fears keep you from leaving?

Have you ever experienced an event that caused you to disconnect from others permanently? How have you reconnected? Or, what's stopping you?

Have you ever been in a negative power relationship? What made you recognize the negativity of the relationship? What caused you to leave this negative sphere of influence? Or, what is prohibiting you from leaving?

What types of people are you uncomfortable around? Is it your unfamiliarity or is it your parental messages that cause you discomfort? What do you need to learn to feel more comfortable around these people?

Chapter Three — Orange Level Energy

Emotional feeling, interactions, sexuality, psychic, social interactions

Give examples from your life of people who use their power positively or negatively. What role did emotion play in each?

Have you ever had a good relationship become strained? What caused it? Did you let the strain build into a wall? How did you change it, or did you?

List the societal rules that influenced you when you were growing up. Do you agree with them today? Why or why not?

How do you view your mistakes: a tragedy or a lesson? How could your mistakes be seen differently by someone else?

Have you ever been around someone who drains your energy, so you feel exhausted? How do you recharge?

Think back: Was there a major event in your life six months to two years prior to a short-term major illness that caused you anger, guilt, resentment, dread, or fear? When you think of that problem, where do you experience tension in your body? Is that where you were ill? How have you overcome those feelings?

Have you ever been depressed? How did you actively change yourself, so your feelings did not become a major depression? If it did become a full-fledged depression, what was the issue you were focusing on at that time? How did you release your depression?

Chapter Four — Yellow Level Energy
Intellect, thinking, planning, linear thinking

Have you ever lied? How did you feel afterwards? What did you have to do to maintain that lie? How would your life have been different if you had not lied? What did you do to rectify the lie?

Are you comfortable making decisions? Were you allowed choices as a child? If not, what did you have to learn to be comfortable making decisions? In what areas are some decisions uncomfortable to make? Why?

Have you ever been around an angry person? Has anyone ever explained that person's background? How would your attitude change if you knew their background?

Have you ever been around negative people who seemed to draw others in? If you were drawn in, what made you decide to leave their sphere of influence? What have you purposely done to avoid being drawn in again?

Chapter Five — Green Level Energy

Family, love, children, balance, nurturing, inner connecting, mother, home

Describe how the highs and lows of life affect you. What do you need to change so they affect you less dramatically?

In what way are your relationships supportive? In what way are they not? Have you told these unsupportive people of your feelings? Where could you find more supportive people?

Did you grow up in a loving, supportive home? If so, how has that affected your current relationships? If not, how has it affected your relationships? What could you do to change them?

What types of fatigue do you feel after each type of travel: air, train, or car? If you have ever had a short ride home after a hospital stay, how did you feel before leaving the hospital and after arriving home? How does being near microwaves, computers, palm pilots, etc., affect you?

Chapter Six — Blue Level Energy

Speaking, knowing, self-confidence, self-knowing, self-love

How have you changed over the last few years? How have you addressed your challenges, become more forgiving, eliminated anger, or accepted yourself and others unconditionally? What more do you have to do?

Are there any animals, plants, or locations that attract you? How does each make you feel?

Give three examples of when you have made wise decisions and three where you have made unwise decisions. Thinking back, describe your self-esteem or the pressures influencing your decisions.

Have you been around charismatic people? How do you feel around them? Did they use their power positively or negatively? If they were negative, what caused you to recognize it? What caused you to leave their sphere of influence?

Have you known people who cannot let go of their children or children who cannot become independent? What kind of separation did you have from your parents? Was it difficult or easy?

Chapter Seven — Indigo Level Energy

Intuition, networking, unity, mass consciousness, universe

List the important factors you use to evaluate people. Once you've evaluated, how do you treat both those with whom you get along and those you do not?

List a few of your family's strong beliefs. Are they valid today? Why or why not? Could others view them as prejudices?

Think of someone who is difficult for you to like. Why don't you like her? Is she too much like you? Do you know her background? Are you afraid or intimidated by her? Why are you unwilling to accept her? Is she richer or poorer than you? What would make you more comfortable around her?

Do you have an addiction to gambling, food, alcohol, exercise, shopping, money, drugs, sex, etc.? What need does your addiction fulfill for you? If you have overcome it, how did you do it?

In the third person, describe your personality. What life events shaped your personality? Where could you improve, so you can progress?

Chapter Eight — Violet Level Energy
Transformation

Often a greater purpose comes from the illnesses of famous people: Rock Hudson and AIDS and Michael J. Fox and Parkinson's disease. List more people you know of, either personally or by reputation, who have turned the awareness of their issues into causes to benefit others.

Notes

Notes

Glossary

Akashic Record - A Hindu belief that each person's soul book is in an ethereal energy library, which holds the records of souls with whom you have connected, your lessons, how you handled them, and all your thoughts and deeds.

Aura - The energy field surrounding the human body.

Astrology - The study of the energy of the planets based on your birth date. It describes your personality and future life challenges.

Chakras - The energy centers of the body, which are situated in the middle of the body over the spinal cord.

Chemical - The chemical emitted from the body, which attracts and connects to others.

Chemistry - Chemistry is an energy exchange between two souls, who were joined in a previous lifetime.

Color - Every color emits energy. We are comprised of energy which is affected by the colors we wear and those in our environment.

Crystals - Crystals are formed from fossilized water and transmit various energies that can affect humans.

Free Will - The doctrine which states that human beings are not physically or divinely controlled in their choices.

Grounding - The act of visually attaching to the Earth and protecting oneself during a meditative session.

Karma - The law which states that the effects of a person's actions determine his fate from lifetime to lifetime.

Life Review - During many near-death experiences, some people experience a moving picture-like review of their entire life that includes all their thoughts, words, and deeds.

Near-Death Experiences - A person dies, experiences various events, and returns to life.

Numerology - Numerology is the study of the numbers of your birth date and name to describe your personality and future life patterns.

Out-of-body Experience - An out-of-body experience occurs when the conscious mind leaves the individual during various situations, both positive and negative, for self-protection or further spiritual work.

Past Lives - The various lives a soul has lived during other incarnations on Earth.

Platonic - The relationship between a man and woman where it is assumed there is no sexual desire.

Predestination – The belief that all your life's challenges were predetermined before manifesting as a human.

Regression - Tapping into the unconscious mind to learn of past experiences from childhood or from previous lives.

Reincarnation - The belief that the soul lives numerous lives in its quest to become unconditionally loving.

Rosicrucians - Members of the fraternal order or brotherhood who utilize their minds and abilities to achieve their wants and needs.

Sadism and Masochism - A sexual act where the individual requires pain and cruelty to feel pleasure. Also known as S and M.

Glossary

Shamanism - A practice from ancient civilizations and cultures of traveling into the spirit world to gather information for advice, guidance, decision-making, problem-solving, healing, and enlightenment.

Soul Retrieval - A ceremony to return parts of the soul lost from physical or psychological trauma, which currently reside in a non-reality state.

Third Eye - A term for your sixth or intuition chakra. It is located just above the space between your eyebrows.

Vision Quest - A Native American practice of personal communication between the individual and spirit.

About the Author

Linda Hargesheimer's life-changing experience, in 1980, began her exploration of spirituality. Over the years, she expanded her knowledge by reading on a variety of subjects, studying with several teachers, and taking spiritual trips to the Yucatan, Egypt, Peru, and Brazil. With the help of a spiritual therapist, she opened in meditation to information for *The Letter of Love*.

Ms. Hargesheimer, a former teacher of children and adults, is the mother of two adult sons. She lives in New England with her husband and golden retriever, Cindi.

Printed in the United States
35774LVS00002B/313-387

9 780976 878834